AND A DEER'S EAR, EAGLE'S SONG, AND BEAR'S GRACE

ANIMALS AND WOMEN

Published in the United States by Cleis Press Inc., P.O. Box 8933, Pittsburgh, Pennsylvania 15221, and P.O. Box 14684, San Francisco, California 94114.

Printed in the United States
Cover design: Cecilia Brunazzi
Typesetting: CaliCo Graphics
Logo art: Juana Alicia

First Edition.
10 9 8 7 6 5 4 3 2 1

Library of Congress Cataloging-in-Publication Data
And a deer's ear, eagle's song and bear's grace : animals and women / edited by Theresa Corrigan & Stephanie T. Hoppe.
  p.   cm.
Includes bibliographical references.
ISBN 0-939416-38-7 : $24.95. — ISBN 0-939416-39-5 (pbk.) : $9.95
  1. Women and animals—Literary collections.   2. American literature—Women authors.   3. American literature—20th century.   4. Animals—Literary collections.   5. Women—Literary collections.
I. Corrigan, Theresa, 1949–.   II. Hoppe, Stephanie T.
PS509.W62A5   1990
810.8'036—dc20   90-40514
                                                                         CIP

Grateful acknowledgment is made to the following for permission to reprint previously published material: *Carol J. Adams*: © 1990 Carol J. Adams; material in this article appears in *The Sexual Politics of Meat: A Feminist-Vegetarian Critical Theory* by Carol J. Adams (New York: Continuum, 1989). Used with permission of Continuum Publishing Co. *Dori Appel*: © 1989 Dori Appel; a slightly different version appeared in *Yankee* (September 1989). *Beth Bosk*: Extrapolated from "Susan Maurer: The spawning channel. Safer sex for salmon"; appeared first in *New Settler Interview* (1988) 29, © 1988 *New Settler Interview*. *Chrystos*: © 1988 Chrystos. From *Not Vanishing* by Chrystos, Press Gang Publishers, Canada, 1988. *Jane Curry*: © 1990 Jane Curry. *Linda Hogan*: "Small Life" © 1980 Linda Hogan; first appeared in *Denver Quarterly* 14:4 (1980). "Waking Up the Rake" © 1988 Linda Hogan; first appeared in *Parabola* 13:2 (1988). *Denise Levertov*: from *Collected Earlier Poems 1940–1960*. Copyright © 1958 by Denise Levertov Goodman. Reprinted by permission of New Directions Publishing Corporation. *Jean Pearson*: © 1989 Jean Pearson. *Marge Piercy*: from MY MOTHER'S BODY by Marge Piercy. Copyright © 1985 by Marge Piercy. Reprinted by permission of Alfred A Knopf Inc. *Elisavietta Ritchie*: An earlier version appeared in *The Christian Science Monitor*, 17 March 1987; © 1987 *The Christian Science Monitor*. Reprinted by permission of the author. *Alix Kates Shulman*: © Alix Kates Shulman 1975; first appeared in *13th Moon* (Winter, 1975). *Mary TallMountain*: © 1974 Mary TallMountain; first appeared in *Hyperion* (April 1974). *Alison Townsend*: Epigraph by Isak Dinesen from *Out of Africa and Shadows on the Grass*, Vintage Books, 1985, © Isak Dinesen 1937, 1960, reprinted by permission of Random House, Inc.

AND A DEER'S EAR, EAGLE'S SONG, AND BEAR'S GRACE

ANIMALS AND WOMEN

EDITED BY THERESA CORRIGAN AND STEPHANIE HOPPE

CLEIS PRESS

PITTSBURGH·SAN FRANCISCO

Contents

Introduction

I. . . . a reminder that all of us living ones are highly perishable and should be cherished while there is time.

II. . . . all with different habits and needs but living in close association.

III. Sing to me the howl of resistance.
Dream to me the forests of your heart.

IV. In our selves and lives it has surely only begun.

Introduction

In these stories—"stories" in a wide sense, the sense in which all writings that give shape to our perceptions, from a child's bedtime story to scientific theories, are stories—women with many years of experience and expertise across a range of fields investigate the nature and implications of our cultural view of animal existence. In fiction, poetry, interviews and nonfiction articles, they assemble from the details of daily life a practical ethic for living—as we have no choice but to live, whether in fear or with understanding—in the natural world, on this Earth, each of us but one of its multifarious and, of necessity, interrelated inhabitants.

This volume forms a companion to and continuation of our anthology *With a Fly's Eye, Whale's Wit, and Woman's Heart*, but each book stands also as an independent whole, as, indeed, each individual piece in both of the books is complete in itself. The pieces also provide context for each other, however, developing themes and resonances of the ultimately seamless web of our perceptions, understanding and interactions. We hope this joint work of ours will find its deepest meaning off the page—as a continuing strand in your and our lives, in that never-ending process of all we take in and give out of ourselves in our deeds and actions.

We wish to thank the many who have contributed to these books—those who appear in these pages as well as others not individually named—who have collectively enabled the actualization, far more wonderfully than we ever dreamt, that summer afternoon in 1987, two women sitting and talking in a green garden, with cats and butterflies and roses and spiders and ants and always more.

Theresa Corrigan and Stephanie T. Hoppe

I.

... a reminder that all of us living ones are highly perishable and should be cherished while there is time.

The Last Wolf
Mary TallMountain

The last wolf hurried toward me
through the ruined city
and I heard his baying echoes
down the steep smashed warrens
of Montgomery Street and past
the few ruby-crowned highrises
left standing
their lighted elevators useless

Passing the flicking red and green
of traffic signals
baying his way eastward
in the mystery of his wild loping gait
closer the sounds in the deadly night
through clutter and rubble of quiet blocks

I heard his voice ascending the hill
and at last his low whine as he came
floor by empty floor to the room
where I sat
in my narrow bed looking west, waiting
I heard him snuffle at the door and
I watched

He trotted across the floor
he laid his long gray muzzle
on the spare white spread
and his eyes burned yellow
his small dotted eyebrows quivered

Yes, I said.
I know what they have done.

Under an October Moon
Lorraine Dale

The sirens stirred an ancient, feral urge within her. She almost raised her head to howl. . . .

There was a howling in the wind, a haunting sensation as it swept the city, ignoring her woolen jacket . . . stripping her naked. . . . Her body screamed and begged to move from the tight, fetal crouch.

The curb was wet and cold. She sneezed and was astounded by the beauty of the wet, clear mucus as it danced from her face and clung, glistening like the wet pavement under the buzzing street lamps, from her nose, her fingertips, her breast.

She sensed movement, chaos growing around her, but could see nothing, nor hear. For the moment the world reached no farther than the sound of her heavy, wheezing breath and the blue-gray smoke that spiraled from the tip of her cigarette.

Cigarettes are poison. Like red meat. And men.

She'd heard that somewhere.

The cigarette continued to reappear on her lips.

She swirled, drawn with each inhalation, down, in . . . as smoke is drawn deeper . . . into another place . . . where she loped through the underbrush strong and proud and sacred . . . a world of honor, of order . . . every participant a willing link in an endless chain . . . no games of torture . . . no needless death, or pain . . . .

Pain! The smoldering butt dropped to the ground. She winced, brought back . . . to a crowd gaping . . . dampness on her buttocks and thighs.

"Whadda ya think? Lover's quarrel?"

"Na—a, she looks like a dyke ta me."

"Yeah . . . ya know how them lesbos are. Hate men."

"Come on, she *can't* be, look at them legs."

"Oh? What else can ya see?"

"Let me have a look, will ya?"

She huddled beneath the long jacket that was her shelter, her only armor against the prying eyes . . . the faces . . . drooling, pushing, necks craning, moving as one now, a huge gelatinous glob, taking on a life of its own, pulsing and rocking, confirming the safety of her detached world . . . .

She remembered . . . .

How she had worn a thick fur coat that shielded her from the brambles, the playful nips of her siblings, and the flashing teeth and claws of her prey . . . .

The joy she had known, ripping open the flesh of her victims, lapping up the warm liquid, tearing muscle, crushing bone . . . .

She felt no joy now.

There were traces of dark, crusted blood under her nails and deep brown patches on her sleeves.

At least she had found her jacket, or someone had.

The rest of her clothes were scraps, still lying where he had shredded them from her body, delighting in her shaking, twitching fear. She *did* remember that.

"Hey, girlie, ya change yer mind at the last minute, or what?"

"Poor guy, why'd ya do it?!"

"Ever seen someone so—cut up? Makes me sick!"

Chatter filtered through in fragments.

His breath had smelled of rotting garbage and cheap wine. The stench remained where his mouth had violated hers. His filthy hands had pushed her head . . . down . . . .

The momentary recollection brought bile up into her throat.

The moon appeared. As the wind pushed a cloud aside, she felt herself lifted from the muck of the city. Floating above, she viewed the scene impassively, peacefully . . . .

Poor man. He had chosen a difficult victim. The young, vulnerable woman he perceived was not as she had seemed to be. Had she been in her body, had she not lost her mind from her body, she would have laughed aloud. The universe has a sense of humor. Dark, perhaps . . . .

The look of terror remained on his face when they pulled the blanket over his head and wheeled him away, his pants still down.

Curiosity waned, and the drifters and the night walkers returned to the shadows as the ambulance pulled away.

She felt a rough hand on her shoulder.

"We'll need to take you in now, Ma'am."

She paused for a moment beneath the October moon. Then, in chorus with the fading sirens, she threw back her head and howled.

To Gallop
Diane de Avalle-Arce

Mary Lynne settled deeper in the saddle, her calf muscles contracted, ankles sharply flexed in worn boots. Her shoulders swayed back a point as the big bay shortened stride. Her fourth finger twitched the taut reins, and the three-quarters of a ton of horseflesh compressed from nose to tail like a bent spring. The big ironshod hooves thudded in the same rhythm as before, but each foot snapped higher and came down in a shorter stride.

She shifted to her right hip with a movement imperceptible to the eye. Her narrow light eyes glanced forward and left; the horse turned at the canter, as smoothly as a sailing ship answering the rudder, and rose in a long parabola clearing a three-foot post-and-rail.

Mary Lynne swayed forward to the impulsion thrusting her up, absorbing the shock of landing in the angle of her knee and ankle. The horse cantered on at the same even pace, easy in his mind, balanced between her hands and legs.

But on the tighter curve heading into the three-six timber wall, he lost cadence. Mary Lynne felt the rising doubt, the beginning of hesitation, not rational but muscular, and squeezed her calves against the short ribs. She flexed the fourth finger of each hand on the reins, briefly, with authority. The big horse bent his hocks well under, gripping the bit for reassurance, and jumped the wall, tucked forehooves clearing the wooden coping neatly.

Good lesson. She dropped the reins on his neck, and he came down to a trot, walk, and halt, stretching out his neck and blowing through his nostrils.

"Good boy, Merry, super horse. Here's for you." She patted the damp shoulder and leaned over it to feed him a stump of carrot as he reached around. The horse munched noisily, dropping specks of orange spume from his bit, and tears started in her eyes because of the power and docility and harmony of her mount, and now she had to get down into the workaday walking world.

She dropped the stirrups and slid to the ground, a long way from the withers of the rangy Thoroughbred. He turned his narrow head and nosed the pocket of her breeches for more carrots. He was a green hunter with a lot of promise; a four-year-old, coming along well, though still a little goosey.

She didn't own him. She got four hundred dollars a month to board him, train him, hunt him with a recognized pack and show locally in the ribbons, so he could bring five figures in Southern Pines in the spring.

Schooling hunters was Mary Lynne's business, had been for thirteen years since she'd ridden ponies too small for adults when she was twelve. She didn't know how to do anything else. In her twenties she was still thin and wiry as a teenager, pale hair tied in a ponytail. Only the pitiless October sun showed up fine dry lines at the corners of her eyes and mouth.

She hung the reins over her shoulder, unhooked the gate of the ring, and walked to the barn with the horse following. There she unsaddled and hosed him down. The dark outline of the saddle on his hide disappeared, the froth under flank and elbow floated away on ripples over the cracked concrete footing. She shut off the faucet and scraped the streaming water down his coat with a brass scraper.

The horse steamed in the sun. As she worked on him, the quarrel of the night before replayed in her mind.

Jack, his brows in a straight line, his face twisted into harsh angles, hunched behind the pull-down table at one end of the trailer's living area. The remaining floor space was piled with tack to clean. The way he put down the handful of bills he was fooling with she knew he was going to be mean.

"What are those filthy boots doing on the living room carpet?"

"It gets dark so early now, and there's no light in the barn."

"All over horseshit. I smell it."

"I don't mind."

"I prefer to have some obvious distinction between the living room and the stables."

"I don't mind." Mary Lynne picked up the other boot.

"You don't mind anything much." Jack didn't yell, ever, but he had an edge like a cross-cut saw to his voice.

"I mind worrying about money all the time."

"Exactly. Which is why this business is failing."

Mary Lynne said, "How much are we short this month?"

"Five hundred and thirteen dollars exactly. That's not making a payment to the feed store."

"Oh."

"And you still haven't done anything about school shoes for Margie."

"It isn't shoes so much," said Mary Lynne. "She's supposed to have sneakers for gym, but they cost twenty dollars."

"So let one of the damned nags go barefoot! Why doesn't Van Dine pay extra for the shoes her airhead horse throws? Or even pay for the fences he breaks?"

"Only three boards, Jack, and you can't—"

"Oak boards at nine sixty-seven each!"

"If you hadn't lost your job, we could—"

"I did *not* lose my job! The company went out of business. Get that through your head. It folded. Bust. Kaput. Do you think I *choose* to be stuck in a twelve-wide mobile home full of horseshit? With less living space than a horse gets?"

He stopped there because ten-year-old Margie was picking her way through the boots, sponges, and newspaper, carrying a paperback copy of *National Velvet*. They were silent until the bathroom door clicked, Jack rigid, Mary Lynne rubbing neat's-foot oil on a bridle.

Jack went on, "This place is such a mess you can't get to the john without risking your neck."

"I'll pick up as soon as I finish."

Jack got up, leaving the bills on the table. He went to the kitchen end and ran the faucet until the water got cold. She heard the clink of a jelly glass and a soft plop—one of her begonia cuttings must have fallen off the sill. She went to pick it up, both she and Jack turning hip-on to pass each other in the narrow space between sink and refrigerator, like a figure in a square dance; a reflex action, no mutual accommodation intended. She noticed the water in his glass was amber-colored.

"Mary Lynne," said Margie coming out of the bathroom,

"Could a girl really ride in the Grand National and win it?" She waved *National Velvet*.

"Not real likely. Have you done your homework?"

"Not all of it."

"Better do it." It was the school that wanted sneakers—Margie would rather have a pair of real riding boots, Mary Lynne would bet.

The child trudged back to her six-by-seven bedroom, trailing the belt of her faded pink bathrobe. She closed the door but the TV could be heard as clearly with the door closed as open.

Mary Lynne had turned on the gas under a saucepan of water, and now it was rolling. She put two spoonfuls of instant in a mug, filled it with water, and added a splat of condensed milk. Sipping scalding thick coffee, she took five steps back to the living area. She put down the mug and picked up her rag.

"Talk about my drinking, when you're doped up with coffee all the time."

Mary Lynne rubbed the bridle with the rag. After a certain point, she never answered. Presently Jack would finish his drink, put away the bills, kiss his daughter goodnight, and go to bed.

Then Mary Lynne would go check the barn as she did every night, and take a solitary long nightwalk around the pasture and woodlot. Last night she'd walked a long way before she could stand to go back to the trailer.

Now she haltered and blanketed the big gelding and turned him into his box. He thrust his head over the door, unwilling to give up her attention, but she had the tack to wipe and put away.

Jack was handsome. The first thing she'd noticed, three—no, four years ago. He was an executive trainee with an electronics firm, and she wouldn't have ever met him at all but that he took Margie for lessons to the riding stable where she taught. Margie was little but she was spunky, up to the best small pony in the barn in no time, and she really took to Mary Lynne.

So Jack started inviting her for a hamburger and Pepsi after the lesson and asking her about her life. He never heard of an Equestrian Science degree, but he thought it was just great. Jack seemed to her like someone from another world, a bright glossy one like a magazine.

She could hardly help being crazy about him. They were married, and Jack wanted a place in the country where she could have her own stable, and Margie could ride all she wanted.

But after he lost his job Jack turned out to have an awful mean streak, and it seemed she couldn't do anything right, especially about Margie.

Mary Lynne didn't like it when someone said Jack married her on the rebound after his first wife left him. She was sure he loved her. But it seemed like he was always expecting something more from her, something she couldn't figure out.

The school bus rumbled down the paved road, paused, and hauled off again. Margie ran into the barn and banged open the tack room.

"Can I ride now, Mary Lynne, can I? Snowdrop's bad leg looks almost like the other one, so can I?"

"Sorry, Margie. Almost isn't good enough. Maybe for the weekend—"

"Ohhhhhh!" Margie gave a long, dramatic moan. "Then can't I ride *at all?*"

"Sure, take Buck as far as you like. He needs it."

"But I never can catch him, and anyway he'll be covered with burrs. Can't I take the filly?"

"No, Margie, you know you aren't allowed to ride the boarders, and that filly'd dump you anyway. She's too goosey."

"No, she isn't. I can ride anything in this whole stupid barn!"

"Why don't you take a pail of oats and a lead rope behind your back where Buck can't see it?"

"He knows that trick by heart!"

"Try it anyway," offered Mary Lynne, pouring Epsom salts into a bucket.

"I'll play with the kittens," Margie announced, shrill with offense. "You'll be sorry!" she added as she slammed the door, but Mary Lynne was running the hose into the bucket then. She dropped an electric heating coil into it; three extension cords plugged together snaked out the window up to the trailer.

When the water was hot, she lugged the bucket out into the corridor and looked around in case Margie wanted to help, but she was nowhere in sight. The kittens were in the hayloft.

Mary Lynne took the bucket into the end stall and stirred it up with her hand. A small Arab mare, ghostly in the half-dark, nickered. Mary Lynne stroked the unclipped fuzzy neck and said, "Shake, Snowdrop," holding out her hand. The mare obediently held up her foreleg. The cut, a nasty jagged tear, was nearly closed; but the leg was thick and hot. Mary Lynne guided it into the bucket. The mare hitched her hindquarters and switched her tail at the first splash, then stood quietly. A half-hour soak, like the vet said, with ten minutes over for luck.

Mary Lynne let her mind drift to nowhere, waiting out the time with the halter in her hand.

Margie didn't appear. Mary Lynne put a steel currycomb in her pocket and went down to the bottom. The underbrush here was overgrown and going to seed, sifting feathered, hooked, winged, and barbed seedcases on the air.

Buck, her old barrel-shaped dun quarter horse, was still sound, but too old to hunt and too ornery for a school horse. He stayed out and stayed fat on wire grass and wild lespedeza. Now, belly deep in a tangle of brambles, honeysuckle, and sumac, he pricked his black ears. Not seeing a rope, he trundled up to her for his carrot.

"Know all the tricks, don't you, old lazybones," she murmured as she went to work on the foxtails in his coat, already long and shaggy against the coming winter. It was peaceful, brushing the old horse, and she took her time. Once she heard a shot. Was Jack home shooting rats in the barn? She wished he wouldn't do that, a bullet could ricochet and hit a horse. Maybe they were squirrel-hunting in the woods on the other side of the road. She shuddered, imagining a small ragged corpse dropping from a tree.

Jack pulled into the barnyard in the twelve-year-old Ford with a .22 across the rear window and a pile of bagged feed in the back. The exhaust spurted thick blue smoke.

The white pony, the brown filly, the chestnut, all poked long inquisitive faces over the stall doors. Another horse cantered along the fence of the turn-out paddock, heavy hindquarters bunching and flattening. The tabby cat stalked down the manure pile with a formal air.

Margie must be watching TV. The big stall was empty, so Mary

Lynne must have taken the expensive one out on the trail.

Jack hefted down the feed sacks and stacked them, arranging in his mind what he was going to say in front of Margie. No job right now—not the furniture company, the department store, the insurance agency, or even the Kwikee-Take-Out; if things got better they were going to give him a call.

The feedstore clerk had said, "Thought I'd just mention in passing, Mr. Thomas, we don't like the accounts to go much over the sixty days."

"Right, I'll see to that."

"How's your little girl?" she added. "Still crazy about horses?"

"Pretty much."

"It must be wonderful for her on the old Holmes place, with Mrs. Thomas a riding teacher and all—"

Jack didn't see why he had to stand around and talk all day, even with an account ninety days past due.

Now he locked the feed room and left the barn. Years ago it must have been trim and white, housing the Holmeses' horses with grooms to take care of them. But the big house had burned in the forties, and now the barn and twenty acres were all that was left, the pasture fences rotten and pieced together with barbed wire.

The rent was low, but it was put-up-and-make-do; the Arab mare, used as a school pony, had cut her leg on the wire and was still laid up. That meant no income from lessons. The vet bill hadn't been paid either. Jack felt like a steel spring wound tighter and tighter as he mentally thumbed through the pile of bills. Vet. Feed. Farrier. Sears and Roebuck. Margie's shoes.

He was about to get into the truck when he saw the rat run. He whipped the rifle off the rack and fired in one quick motion, but missed. He muttered, "Shit," and waited a moment, holding the gun. "Even the rats are getting out."

The echoes of the shot died, and he heard the beat of hooves coming down the hill pasture—coming too fast. Mary Lynne never galloped a horse home. He shaded his eyes and looked against the sun. Down a long green-gold slope hurtled a big young horse, Merry Widow at full stretch. He was going too fast, unbalanced, bolting.

"He'll break another damn fence," thought Jack. Then, with a sickening jolt, he saw the rider's red pigtails: it was Margie.

He didn't know if she tried to pull the horse up and couldn't, or if she was showing off all the way. They hurtled down the hill like a steeplechase; it was clear the horse had to jump the five-foot timber fence on the road, because he couldn't stop.

He rose gamely at it, Margie clinging to his neck, and for a moment, with the pair fused into one against the red sunset sky, Jack thought they'd make it.

But the fence was too high and the oak rail was new. It held, and Merry Widow turned a cartwheel into the road, the tiny figure of Margie coming down with him on the pavement.

Jack was already running on the farm road, running slowly, leadfooted, no air in his lungs, while the big colt scrambled up splay-legged and trembling, but Margie lay in a huddle and never moved or made a sound.

Mary Lynne heard him shouting and called the Rescue Squad. She followed him and the ambulance in the pickup. Jack didn't say a word in the ER, just smoked walking up and down until the doctor came out and told them. She couldn't stop crying, not only because Margie was dead, and she was just a little kid, but also because Jack looked so dreadful. And what would happen now?

She started to run, down the long bright corridor smelling of antiseptic, but Jack caught her by the elbow and made her get in the pickup and he drove home.

The funeral was three days later. Neither of them had been to church since their wedding, when Margie was flower girl in a blue taffeta dress to go with her hair, and so proud of it. Mary Lynne wondered if Jack was thinking about that. He looked handsome and distant in a suit and tie, but unnaturally pale, the sharp line of his fresh haircut startling against his skin. He stared straight ahead the whole time. Mary Lynne wanted to take his hand in the cemetery, but he had them clasped tightly behind his back.

The service wasn't long. On the way home, Jack said, "She would have been eleven in three weeks exactly."

"She was an awfully good rider for her age," said Mary Lynne, and Jack didn't answer.

They returned alone from the funeral, just as they'd kept pretty much to themselves after Jack lost his job. But a neighbor had left a pineapple upside-down cake on the step, from which Mary Lynne cut two slices, wrapping the rest in plastic wrap. She made a tunafish salad.

Jack poured himself a drink. Mary Lynne pulled down the table and set out two paper plates with tunafish sandwiches, paper napkins, two glasses of iced tea, and the slices of cake in the middle. Jack came to the table and sat, but he didn't eat.

"That horse ought to be shot," he announced.

"Oh, Jack, you know it was an accident—"

"Accident, hell."

"Don't you want any lunch?" Mary Lynne offered the plate of cake over the uneaten sandwich.

"Why did you let her ride that horse?"

"I didn't! I said she could take Buck—"

"You should have kept an eye on her!"

"Are you blaming me for the accident?" Mary Lynne asked, because she couldn't believe it.

"It happened, didn't it?" Jack finished his drink and got up. "I guess you're to blame." He went out and opened the hood of the pickup. He tinkered with it for a couple of hours, finishing the bourbon, and went deer-hunting.

It was a steely November day, perfect for scent. The low clouds were pewter-colored, and a sharp little wind veered between west and north. The foxhounds, all calico patches and waving tails, ran about nosing the dun-colored stubble in the meadow. The huntsman walked his hogged half-bred chestnut around them; the Master sat stationary on his massive old black hunter and accepted respectful greetings from the field.

Mary Lynne had Merry out for his first hunt, moving him in circles to occupy his mind. The pupil on Snowdrop gripped the reins so tightly the pony fussed and chucked her head, sidling after the big bay gelding.

"Slack off on her mouth and sit up straight, Shelia," Mary Lynne advised.

"She always follows Merry," whined Shelia.

"Take her over where your mother is, so she can present you to the Master. Mind everyone's heels."

"Okay." Shelia jagged on the pony's mouth, booted her in the ribs, and jolted off at a ragged trot. Mary Lynne sighed for Snowdrop, but her mind was chiefly on calming the volatile Thoroughbred and keeping him out of trouble.

The huntsman called up the hounds and jogged towards the near covert, the pack like a crazy quilt spread out around him. Merry Widow pulled hard, half rearing, and she got him back in hand just in time to move off with the field, bay and grey and chestnut, red coats, black coats, children's tweeds and gaiters, behind the Master.

Hounds crossed a line at once. Reveille gave tongue. The huntsman cocked his head, then set on the rest of the pack with high-pitched yips in bastard Norman French. "*Loo* in, Raleigh! *Loo* in, Ranger!" The Master picked up a sedate hand-gallop.

The field followed, Merry Widow fighting for his head. Mary Lynne gave and took, gave and took, with her thin strong hands, coaxing him down and back. Ahead was a line of gold and black trees, Sligh's woodlot: foxes always made for it, but it was too small for them to lose the hounds.

Jack was deer-hunting, alone. He liked to still-hunt, picking a likely place and waiting until a deer crossed. He looked down on weekend deer-hunters, their dogs, their six-packs and their yackety-yak: Jack hunted for a fat buck in the freezer, not a party. He heard foxhounds in the bottom. Damn fools, what good was a fox? But the racket might spook a deer, might send him up on the ridge into the gunsights. Grackles squawked in protest. Jack slipped back the safety.

He settled into a clump of elderberry and emptied his mind of everything but the shape of a buck at the cross hairs. When a real deer filled the outline in his imagination, his finger would squeeze the trigger between one heartbeat and another. A hundred pounds of venison and no bill to pay. Think of that— think of the deer in the gunsight, the dream deer of longing. The real deer is somewhere, coming closer to merge with the silhouette in the mind's eye.

Think of the deer, don't think of Margie, redhead Margie who ran to meet him, don't ever think of Margie again. Her mother didn't think of her, just walked out; Mary Lynne takes care of the horses, but she didn't mind Margie. Now there was no Margie to mind. Don't think. Don't think at all. See the deer, the dream shape becoming real in the sights of the gun, feel the finger tighten on the trigger.

The field skirted the woods, jumped a ditch, and clattered over the state road. Merry Widow shied at a culvert, but waited his turn; Mary Lynne was glad to see Snowdrop, a flash of white, ahead. Hounds checked briefly in thick underbrush, then poured out of Sligh's woods yelling. The field moved off.

Mary Lynne's mood lightened. She could let the horse out a little. You needed a horse that would go well in front to fetch any kind of a price in Southern Pines. She let him lengthen stride, moving ahead easily, ears pricked to the baying of hounds.

The sun broke through the clouds and turned the cutover stubble to pale gold, burnishing the horses' clipped satiny coats. Deer-hunters in orange vests waved and watched them pass.

Merry Widow took a stiff post-and-rail in stride. "Good boy," Mary Lynne murmured, patting the warm slick shoulder. The horse snorted, galloping strongly and steadily, doing what he was bred for. The wind blew past her ears, cutting off everything but the cry of the hounds. The other riders were strung out and scattered behind. Margie's accident, Jack's black moods, the debts, all that was behind.

The cry of the pack shifted downwind; the fox was probably making for Oak Grove. There was Taylor's Mill Creek to cross, and Merry wasn't good in bogs. He'd throw a shoe. But they could bear left and hit the creek a half-mile upstream for a clean jump. Mary Lynne rocked back in the saddle, right heel behind the girth and left heel pressed into it.

They cantered by themselves along the line of the ridge for ten minutes; it was broken at last by the narrow creek. Here the slope shelved off abruptly, and Mary Lynne collected the horse with legs, hands, and voice.

As he jumped, she heard a sharp *crack* like a dry stick snapping; the horse fell away under her and slammed hard into the lip of the bank. They both fell back into the creek. She rolled away from the horse's hind legs thrashing in the water and tried to stand, but slipped on the wet clay and slid back.

There was someone, outlined against the sky, on the ridge

above the creek bed. Mary Lynne started to claw herself upright.

It was Jack. Mary Lynne held still, water inches from her mouth. The horse was quiet now. Jack didn't move either. Not quite fainting, she smelled red clay and blood and cordite. Jack was standing above her, too far to see his face. He had shot at her, shot Merry Widow.

She held her breath. Would he shoot again? Would he come down? Did he think she was dead, and would he be sorry later?

Pebbles scrunched. Footsteps got farther away till she couldn't hear them anymore. She lay still, colder and colder, not sure if she could get up, not sure if Jack was waiting up there.

Finally, she got up, sick and shivering. The horse was stiffening, one open eye turned up so the white showed. It seemed like any carcass—she couldn't remember if it had had a name.

She clambered up the ridge and looked around. There was no one in sight and she could not hear hounds. A cardinal perched in a scrubby locust tree, and a red-tailed hawk sailed down the wind; the raw wind dried the red clay on her clothes and face. She was cold but for a burning across the top of her thigh. She pulled apart the rip in her breeches: a blue hole and a larger, purple-red one marked two ends of a dark tunnel through the flesh.

She was shot—he really shot her. She said this to herself many times. Trembling with a rhythmic shiver, she hugged her ribs. She could not think of anything at all to do.

Then she saw a riderless horse trotting uphill. It was Snowdrop, brushing through the stiff garnet-red umbels of sumac, a broken rein trailing, and one stirrup slatting against the saddle. She must have broken loose and followed her stablemate.

The pony came to her and nuzzled her pockets. Mary Lynne automatically felt down the foreleg to the wire cut, then knotted the broken rein and mounted. She threw the useless stirrup over the pommel.

It was late and cold. The red-orange harvest moon rose enormous out of low clouds, floodlighting the mare as she circled nervously. The familiar country looked strange and unknown. Mary Lynne's will wavered like a demagnetized compass needle, and the mare wavered with her.

Then Snowdrop smelled the carcass and panic took her. She

threw up her head and bolted. Mary Lynne's legs clamped to the heaving ribs, she crouched over the streaming mane and rode—rode on, a breakneck pace, a girthbusting point-to-point, a cross-country race. The mare bounded like a hunted deer, and the faster she ran, the harder Mary Lynne rode, on and on under the low clouds toward the distant line of trees, over sedge and scrub, hillocks and hollows.

Iron shoes struck momentary sparks from the pebbles, the mare's wide nostrils showed a red lining as she flew the gullies in the orange light.

Mary Lynne sank lower on her neck, urging her on, on and on, in the cruel November dusk that rose from the folds of the hills. As night closed, they fled the lights of houses, the white lines painted on paved roads.

At the Movies
Amy Edgington

*Dedicated to the memory of Dian Fossey, who spent eighteen years studying
and protecting one of the few remaining populations of mountain gorillas,
in the Virunga range in East Africa. Her deep rapport with animals led
her to become one of the most militant and controversial figures in the
conservation movement. She was murdered in her camp by an unknown
assailant on December 28, 1985.*

O n the movie screen
Digit dies again and Dian
becomes a star.
I sit in the dark
and see the real Dian
with wooly hair
and button-brown eyes
that in death become
as cryptic as an animal's.
Oh, we have our records
of her passion for her own,
her threat charges and her bluffs,
but now she has stopped arguing.
Dian, I don't know why the others are here—
most are probably tourists;
a few may hold a degree of scientific interest;
some will try to shoot down your reputation—
but I want you to know I am
climbing, climbing until my chest hurts
through the mists and nettles,
slipping in shit and mud,
to get as close to you as possible.
I am not afraid, in spite of all I'm told
about how mean and mad you were,
about how you cared too much

and lost your head because of it.
When I catch a glimpse of you and Digit,
side by side, hand in hand,
I mumble in awe, *Surely*
these are both my kin.

Wings of a Wild Goose
Chrystos

for Dian Million

A hen, one who could have brought more geese, a female,
                                           a wild one
dead   Shot by an excited ignorant young blond boy, his first
His mother threw the wings in the garbage   I rinsed them
brought them home, hung them spread wide on my studio wall
A reminder of so much, saving what I can't bear to be wasted
Wings
I dream of wings which carry me far above human bitterness
human walls   A goose who will have no more tiny pale fluttering
goslings to bring alive   to shelter   to feed   to watch fly
off on new wings   different winds
He has a lawn this boy   A pretty face which was recently paid
thousands of dollars to be in a television commercial   I clean
their house every Wednesday morning
2 dogs which no one brushes   flying hair everywhere
A black rabbit who is almost always out of
water   usually in a filthy cage   I've cleaned the cage
out of sympathy a few times although it is not part of what
are called my duties   I check the water as soon as I arrive
This rabbit & those dogs are the boy's pets   He is very lazy
He watches television constantly leaving the sofa in the den
littered with food wrappers, soda cans, empty cereal bowls
If I'm still there when he comes home, he is rude to me   If he
has his friends with him, he makes fun of me behind my back
I muse on how he will always think of the woods
as an exciting place to kill   This family of three lives
on a five acre farm   They raise no crops   not even their own
vegetables or animals for slaughter   His father is a neurosurgeon
who longs to be a poet   His mother frantically searches

31

for christian enlightenment   I'm sad for her   though I don't like
her   because I know she won't find any   The boy does nothing
around the house without being paid   I'm 38 & still
haven't saved the amount of money he has in a passbook found
in the pillows of the couch under gum wrappers   That dead goose
This boy will probably never understand that it is not right
to take without giving   He doesn't know how to give   His mother
who cleaned & cooked the goose says she doesn't really like
to do it but can't understand why she should feel any different
about the goose than a chicken or hamburger from the
supermarket
I bite my tongue & nod   I could explain to her that meat raised
for slaughter is very different than meat taken from the woods
where so few wild beings survive   That her ancestors are
responsible for the emptiness of this land   That lawns feed no
one   that fallow land lined with fences is sinful   That hungry
people need the food they could be growing   That spirituality
is not separate from food or wildness or respect or giving
But she already doesn't like me   because she suspects me
of reading her husband's poetry books when no one is around
& she's right   I do   I need the 32 dollars a week tolerating
them provides me   I wait for the wings on my wall to speak to me
guide my hungers   teach me winds I can't reach   I keep
these wings because walls are so hard   wildness so rare   because
ignorance must be remembered   because I am female   because
I fly

only in my dreams   because I too
will have no young to let go

To the Snake
Denise Levertov

G reen Snake, when I hung you round my neck
and stroked your cold, pulsing throat
        as you hissed to me, glinting
arrowy gold scales, and I felt
        the weight of you on my shoulders,
and the whispering silver of your dryness
        sounded close at my ears—

Green Snake—I swore to my companions that certainly
        you were harmless! But truly
I had no certainty, and no hope, only desiring
        to hold you, for that joy,
                        which left
a long wake of pleasure, as the leaves moved
and you faded into the pattern
of grass and shadows, and I returned
smiling and haunted, to a dark morning.

Whale and Woman

Susan Stinson

Whale:

I see one of you swimming far out. She is floating on her back, as if to give birth, but the water is far too deep for that. Her belly is up, not without its small softness.

I'm interested. There is more hair on that little slip of meat than my whole pod could collect if we each shaved our chin whiskers on coral and let the wisps fall in one place and pile up. The sea would sweep them away with its first impulse of water, but I can entertain the thought. Still, she has less fur than a sea otter and does not look warm.

She exudes human bravado. "An elephant weighs about the same as your tongue," she says.

I go deep. It's a nervous reaction. The breath is first, breath after breath until it becomes not breath but a rush of air that sucks out my lungs, not through my blowholes back to the outer world with that wordy squid in it, but through warmer passages, charting my head until it gathers in cavities, gaseous, waiting for use.

My lungs collapse. I dive. The arch of my back splits the top of the water in the first great curve. I don't know where she's been swept to. My tail rises. I stretch it, lifting my flukes at a sail's angle to the water. There are shores with trees where we winter. I feel kin to the trees and hear the belly voice that tells me rooted things were the food of my mothers before they came back to the water. I'm a stalk in the air even as my bulk makes itself a sea root. Then my tail, too, passes in.

I brush things going down: fish, seaweed, shells, floating crabs. The passing water is soft. It soothes me. Some of my barnacles loosen in the motion. I listen as I move. I hear squeaks and chirps through the first fish layers. Nothing goes silent for me, since I'm a grazer, not a hunter. My heart slows. I barely feel the pressure. My blood itself goes deeper, flowing away from my surfaces, through my fat in rivers, concentrating in my brain and my heart. I pull oxygen from my blood as it travels, and from my muscles; little from my lungs.

I talk about my body because most humans are so ignorant. You don't know much of what you should about the varieties of motion and stillness, or pain, or breathing, or dreaming, or any of the other essential processes of the body.

I hear her as I come back up. It's a stationary rhythm. She moves her arms in the water. I tilt my body to see her. From underneath, she looks like a dark blotch on the hazy surface of light. I pass below her, then surface. White water comes with me. I spout. My stale air rises and hangs as a mist.

I breathe, float, rest, close, then dive again, shallow this time. I turn. I break the surface. I breach. I am in the air. Water streams off me, becoming foam. Parasites drop from my skin. I experience two elements with that lift into the air, then look down at the woman. I see her bobbing and struggling, thrown by my wake. She is shivering, tiny, isolate. I understand all that, even before I hit the water, because I have also been a creature of the surface.

Woman:

It is the language of the body. I know she understood me. I didn't speak with my mouth. It was more reaction: my teeth shook, my body arched in the water, my face changed shape. None of this is silent. She heard what I meant. She has outer ears the size of a pencil lead, one above each eye, but her hearing is acute. I reacted. I told her my idea of tongue and my idea of elephant, and she got it right away. She dove. Her body breaking the water was a wave, slipping under grey skin.

I weigh more wet, but I feel light. I found that out in the tub. Most days I never touch earth, am barely out in the air, get nowhere near fire, but I always take my time in water. I play games. I stick my toes in the faucet or set up a rhythm, moving my body to move the water. My fat is loose, almost liquid. I can feel the waves in the skin of my belly. I shimmer. I wash. I roll the cake of soap over and over between my palms. The soap starts out gold, but works up white. I make mounds of lather. I spread it over me: soft belly circled, soft legs, bent knees. I look at one knee. It rises in the steam, firm at the center and soft out each side, with the lines of a pear. I rinse it, specific fruit. Dip. Splash. Stroke.

I need the tub to hold the water to keep it with me.

Whale:

I can see she is pretending to be a continent. It's hard to banter sizes. She's so tiny, but her whole way of floating says island belly, hillbelly, white water belly, white water thighs. Like flounders say flat and urchins say prickly. It's all over her.

Woman:

Hey, lard ass. Hey, tub of lard. You're fat; did you know that, fatso? Over here, fatty. Hey, fatty. Look at that tub of blubber move. It's disgusting. Let's harpoon her and put her out of her misery.

Whale:

They chatter like that when they're frightened. She's getting cold, and her suit is riding up. She's rippling like the water. It's a pity she's so slight. She's got no place to save her warmth. She's a bone bowl. Don't ask what I know of bowls. Our dead have been carved often enough.

Woman:

I could make catfood out of you. I think kitty would like a nice seafood platter. I could turn you into crayons. You burn good. Something in your guts smells good.

I've got helicopters back there. You didn't see the boat. I've got cannons. I've got harpoons that would feel like just a slight prick going in, then explode deep inside you. Your fat is two feet deep, but I could get past that. Then we'd pump you full of air, compressed air that we've got in tanks on board, and you couldn't even sink. We'd pull you along behind us like a rubber ducky until we felt like stripping you and cutting you up. I could do all that. I'm human.

Whale:

Does she think I want to eat her? Is that what all the agitation is about? But we're swimming in krill. It's a pasture. No, landling, I couldn't digest you without great pain to us both. I don't chew, but your bones would break fitting down my throat. I don't want you in me. What do you want?

Woman:

It's the lard, the fat. We're both fat. We have that condition of the body in common. That's what brought me here.

Whale:

The light is dark in the water. There's no weight to it. It is also important that my body is dark. Myoglobin brings me some of my darkness and holds oxygen in my muscles, so I can use it when I need it as I dive.

Woman:

I'm pale. But can you hear my heart? It's going slow.

Whale:

You can't stay under. You don't have the apparatus.

Woman:

You hear me clearly?

Whale:

Yes, I read your body. It says: fat floats, drips, body drips, flop, fat surge, falls off sides, collops, fat pours, deep fat singing, fat dancing on the water.

Hard to believe something so lovely is floating up from your cramped frame, after all of that ugliness earlier.

Woman:

I had to speak of weapons. They were between us. The violence of my species marks me. I can't help but bring bits of it with me.

Whale:

Have you survived harpooning? I don't see scars.

Woman:

No actual cuts, just constant hate. For instance, I'm sitting on a bus and some girls in the back shout, "She's been eating too many hamburgers. There's half a hamburger sticking out of her ass." Or I read an ad that says, "I lost thirty pounds and rejoined the human race." People wish I wasn't one of them. So I came to find you.

Whale:

I do not feel much link with you. I feel only your desire.

Woman:

I would swell up like a soaked bean if I died in the water. You whales stay warm three days after death. It's all the fat.

Whale:

Yes, I see your little belly. I see the small waves in your back. They are as unremarkable on you as they are on a walrus, a polar bear, a dugong. Why are they so crucial to you?

Woman:

We all know that you're majestic.

Whale:

What a stilted movement. Go on and brush against me if you want contact. Fish do.

Woman:

You could hit me with your flukes.

Whale:

Be afraid, then. I'm bored.

Woman:

Your mouth is wide. I can smell your spout. It makes a mist on my skin.

Whale:

There are limits to this. I must feed and move. You have to rest. Go to your boat. I have other things to hear.

Woman:

Wait. Have you considered a girdle?

Whale:

That's a nasty gesture. Do you find yourself sick of your limbs?

Woman:

How about a diet?

Whale:

What are you talking about? What do you want?

Woman:

It's just that you're so beautiful. It's almost unbearable.

Whale:

Yes.

Woman:

Yes. Even most of my species can see it. But they see me as repulsive.

Whale:

You move with confusion.

Woman:

I'm fat, wet, cold, and alone.

Whale:

Things grow on me in my folded places. That's some company.

Woman:

There must be icicles in this water. I'll come closer.

Whale:

You may stroke me. Just be careful of the lampreys. I barely notice their bites, but you would feel them.

Woman:

We're both so lovely together like this.

Whale:

I like this. You have a full touch. I'm always talking to things against me in the water.

Woman:

Too bad fish don't have hands.

Whale:

I'm no fish. You're trembling.

Woman:

You feel beautiful.

Whale:

Maybe, if you practice holding your breath . . .

Woman:

I've been holding my breath all my life.

Whale:

. . . you could learn to dive.

Sleeping with Cats
Marge Piercy

I am at once source
and sink of heat: giver
and taker. I am a vast
soft mountain of slow breathing.
The smells I exude soothe them:
the lingering odor of sex,
of soap, even of perfume,
its afteraroma sunk into skin
mingling with sweat and the traces
of food and drink.

They are curled into flowers
of fur, they are coiled
hot seashells of flesh
in my armpit, around my head
a dark sighing halo.
They are plastered to my side,
a poultice fixing sore muscles
better than a heating pad.
They snuggle up to my sex
purring. They embrace my feet.

Some cats I place like a pillow.
In the morning they rest where
I arranged them, still sleeping.
Some cats start at my head
and end between my legs
like a textbook lover. Some
slip out to prowl the living room

patrolling, restive, then
leap back to fight about
hegemony over my knees.

Every one of them cares
passionately where they sleep
and with whom.
Sleeping together is a euphemism
for people but tantamount
to marriage for cats.
Mammals together we snuggle
and snore through the cold nights
while the stars swing round
the pole and the great horned
owl hunts for flesh like ours.

A Double Life
Dori Appel

A girl who loved horses thought
she was a horse. Her brown hair
she thought was a mane, her brown
shoes that laced were her hooves,
her neck, not long, became long
when she thought about who she was.
She told no one. When they called
her for suppper she came at an
obedient trot and tucked her napkin
into her shirtfront where the
martingale had chafed when she was
young and wild. When they took her places
she walked properly and answered
courteously, and thought about
the sweet grass in the field where
she greeted the morning, and the moonlight
in the meadow where she ran at night
when everyone was sleeping, and only she
in all the world was awake to the
night sounds and the night shadows,
her hooves bright as stars,
her long neck arcing towards the moon.

Beating the Dog
Judith Barrington

She lowered her belly into heather
and froze. Her nose explored
the breeze, sorted smells of weather
from what mattered. I saw how her eyes stared.

She was so young then, downwind
from two sheep on a hillside purple under blue;
there were farmers with guns in my mind
as I yelled NO. I was young too.

It was no use, my yelling.
The sheep lifted their heads too high
and bolted, swerving, almost falling
over tussocks, while the sky

tilted and spun as I ran,
the dog ran, we barked and yelled
and the four of us, alone up there,
ploughed through bracken and hare-bells.

She heard me at last, left
the sheep heaving and bleating
by a gorse bush. Her eyes softened,
she crouched, and then I was beating

the dog with the leash,
farmers and guns
in my mind as rage washed
over the hill like a storm's hot wind.

I remember how she screamed twice
before I sank down in the heather.
It doesn't matter that she licked my face—
the sorry tears; it doesn't matter

that she barked and skipped through the stream
or that she never stared that way
at a sheep again. Ends and means.
How could things be simple after that day?

Old Bones
Brenda Weathers

Though the dog had been dead for some time the old woman still thought of her and, at times, even imagined she saw the grizzled old bulldog out of the corner of her eye or on entering a darkened room.

At the time the dog died, the two of them had lived many years together in a house with print curtains on the windows and clean but faded linoleum on the floors. Eventually, they had come to resemble one another. Some might have taken offense at being compared to a bulldog. But not she. She felt, in fact, quite complimented, for the dog was, without question, the most unobtrusively loyal, genuinely spontaneous individual of her acquaintance. The woman took wise counsel from animals of all sorts and knew many people would do well to emulate them.

If the woman's chin sagged and her skin hung in folds at her neck—what of it? She owed nothing to anyone, not even an accounting of her appearance and would call no one her better.

As time went on, both woman and dog had an almost identical droop to their eyelids, and each walked with the stiff rolling gait of advanced arthritis.

Though she had named the dog Lily after her favorite flower and because of the incongruity of such a name attached to such a face, in later years she came to call the dog Old Bones. "Old Bones," she would say, "Come on." And Old Bones would, if she had a mind to.

Not young herself when the dog, then a puppy, came to live with her, the woman and the dog got along famously from the very beginning. She had seen the pup's mother at the county fair, all rolls and softness like a dumpling just dropped into the broth, and later went to see the pups. No sooner had she sat in an old platform rocker than one of the pups ran to her, wagging its tail and looking up at her with cocked head and huge brown eyes. The pup seemed to pant at the woman's shoes, perfect for chewing, and at the slight scent of pot roast, which would mean a bone every Sunday.

The woman thought the brindle markings on the pup's white rump resembled little pantaloons, and seldom had she seen anything so cute as the jowled and wizened bulldog face attached to the fat pink-skinned puppy. She wrote a check, stuffed the overjoyed and triumphant pup into her woven bag, and went home.

She lived on a country road just far enough outside a small town that she achieved the benefits of country living. Her house was old and drafty, but it suited her—even with the cold feet and runny nose that winter brought. They were a small price to pay, she would remark, for the joys of her own orchard, acres of woods, and a field large enough for a horse and several goats.

Had she had more money, she could have repaired the leaky sills and drafty attic, but what little extra cash she found went to other purposes. She fed herself and her animals very well, and with any spare cash, she repaired torn fencing or built new sheds.

She enjoyed living in a house occupied by so many before her even as much as she enjoyed the rural setting. She appreciated being just another in the ebb and flow of life played out within the old walls and high plaster ceilings. She often fancied she knew much about the lives of those who had lived here before her just from her hunches or her dreams though she possessed not one shred of factual information.

More than once she had seen the faint image of a young girl sitting in the window seat, and she knew, because she had dreamt it, that an old woman with long hair and high cheekbones had planted those peach trees in the orchard. Believing as strongly as she did in the afterlife made these images as commonplace to her as a wedge of crumb cake or a jar of her own pickled plums.

She had her own views on animal raising as well, which she practiced without so much as a nod in the direction of more conventional thinking. Always, on bringing home a new dog or cat, she would hold the little animal on her lap and stroke its fur. "I'm delighted to get to know you," she would say. "You are free to become who you are and I'll do little to stand in your way." She felt it a sacrilege to expect an animal to obey foolish commands purely for the entertainment of people and detested the sight of some poor dog balancing on its hindquarters and begging for a biscuit. Leftovers were shared equally and neither woman nor animal responded without question to the word NO.

Not all people took well to what some considered an untrained animal, but they were seldom invited back to the old house on the country road.

Though a fading beauty with a fading interest in such matters, the woman had lovers off and on, the more sensitive of these intuiting at once that whatever relationship they might develop with the woman would most certainly be secondary to the one between her and the dog.

Only once had this pattern been broken. In almost every life one comes along and breaks all the patterns and, in doing so, often breaks the heart as well. Just when the woman thought she was finally finished with such distractions as love and passion, a person appeared in her life and set it aflame.

There were problems, of course, as there always are with those who sparkle so. Not the least of the problems involved the lover's beliefs about dogs: sofas and beds were for human occupancy only, and an evening together was too short for scratching behind a fat ear or playing catch with a red rubber ball.

One evening, the couple settled in front of the potbellied stove to enjoy a cup of after-supper coffee. Again and again the dog lumbered over to drop the none-too-clean ball onto the lover's lap suggesting, of course, that they get to know each other a little better.

Finally, the lover stood up and announced, "The dog goes or I do!"

The woman looked first at the lover, the object of such unbridled and unexpected passion and then for a long moment at the animal.

In the end, it was the lover, not the dog who went away—just disappeared one day never to return. In the painful weeks and months that followed, when winter wind swept through the chinks in the walls and loneliness crept from its dusty lurking places, it was the dog and not the lover who offered a warm back to sleep against, a greeting on return from town, and companionship by an evening's fire.

The years went on, and there were no more lovers, but there was always Old Bones, and the two of them came to value their aloneness together and to wish for no other life.

But as the years passed, so too passed the health of youth. One day, the woman realized Old Bones could no longer hear. The many cats noticed first. In fact, it was the phalanx of cats the woman noticed surrounding the dog that gave her the clue.

Old Bones would amble slowly, painfully it seemed, down the dirt drive amid a bevy of cats. When the dog stopped to sniff the air or stare into the distance at something of interest and visibile only to her, the cats stopped too and waited. When the dog resumed, the cats moved with her, leaping back and forth over the dog's broad back, cavorting before her on the drive always directing her attention away from the dangerous road.

The woman smiled where she watched from her window or the porch. There goes Old Bones, she would say to herself. There goes Old Bones with her "hear cats."

The woman continued to speak to Old Bones because she knew that animals hear not only from mouth to ear but from heart to heart as well. "Old Bones," she would still call. "Old Bones, come along." Or, "Old Bones, come and sit with me awhile." And Old Bones always did.

One bright afternoon in late summer, in the dog's fourteenth year, the woman looked out of the window and saw Old Bones asleep in the shade of a tree laden with plump ripe peaches. She smiled and turned away to finish putting up jars of corn she had picked fresh from the garden that morning. When she was done, she wiped her hands on a checkered dishtowel and went again to the window. Old Bones lay as before, in the same place and the same position.

For a long time, the woman stared out the window at her friend, wishing to hold onto those last moments before the certainty of something painful rushed in to blot out all else.

Later in the evening, when it was cooler, she buried Old Bones next to the orchard, then sat by her for a very long time letting her tears fall unashamedly onto the turned earth.

A few years later, on an almost identical summer day, the woman, hair now white and face dried and cracked by age, limped into the orchard to pick peaches. As she gathered fallen peaches and placed them in her apron, she noticed how unusually bright the afternoon light was. Brighter than she had ever seen. The peaches felt uncommonly heavy; she was forced to let them fall back to the ground as she struggled against the dazzling light and a loud, but not unpleasant, ringing about her head. In a moment, or an eternity, she couldn't be sure, she breathed the smell of sun-sweetened grass, dimly aware that she lay with her face pressed into a clump of dark pungent green.

The peach trees faded and with them the grass and the noise, dissolving into golden light. Pain seemed not to matter in the silence of such beauty as she could never have imagined. Then, from deep within the silence, she heard a voice, soft and melodious, call to her. "Old Bones," she heard. "Old Bones, come on."

II.

. . . all with different habits and needs but living in close association.

Small Life

Linda Hogan

I surrender to them all
the arcana of insects
pale stomachs to windows,
gold powder that lets wings fly.
Insects singing
made of light and dust
and children too
innocent between white sheets
that curtain them from night.
Their breath is the song of air.

I give in
to the speck of blood
on the ceiling
that grows into a fly.
And on floors
what wonders in the dark
when light and soft thumps go out
of windows.
The roach
its shining back
and hair thin feet
creaks the tiles
night's music
which means we are safe
we are never alone.

The Cockroach Hovered Like a Dirigible

Elisavietta Ritchie

I don't think I grew up with cockroaches. Perhaps I've forgotten, and we merely co-existed in the various apartments and houses of my childhood.

My mother's attitude toward bugs was not as malevolent as that of some mothers. Although in college she had concentrated on piano, art history, Latin and French, and at twenty-five won a national playwriting award, by thirty-five she was in Guatemala collecting boxes of insects for Chicago's Field Museum. In my parents' sojourns in the Philippines, France, Japan, Cyprus, Lebanon, Portugal, Spain, Thailand, Nigeria, the Virgin Islands, as well as less exotic Chicago, Philadelphia, New York, Washington, and finally, Coconut Grove, Florida, although not scientists, they had ample chance for entomological investigations. I don't remember complaints about bugs and grew up regarding insects with curiosity.

Still, I find mosquitos and flies annoying and wasps terrifying. Recently, however, moving into a ramshackle farmhouse where wasps and many other species settled before we did, I've learned a limited laissez-faire. And I get lost for hours in insect books, all the Latin monikers and homier common names: aquatic pyralidid moth, pale-legged tree-fungus beetle, two-tooth longhorn, constricted flowerbug, brush-footed fritillary—the stuff of poetry, although a sharp editor would blue-pencil the surfeit of adjectives.

Only at twenty-eight did I meet cockroaches I remember—and they were memorable. We had just moved to Washington. At a dinner party in historic Georgetown, with a grand gesture our host lighted the candles on the table, and lo, the walls danced an avant-garde ballet of jointed legs and graceful antennae.

"The best houses in Georgetown," said my mother, "have roaches."

Or, as poet Elizabeth Follin-Jones updated it, "The best roaches have houses in Georgetown."

Farther out in Cleveland Park, we entertained May beetles, June bugs, ants in July, yellow jackets in August, crickets in September. Sometimes too many. But no roaches.

Meanwhile my own children were developing interests in insects. At age six, Alexander brought me a miniature tyrannosaurus: grey armor crenelated, arched and spiked, elbows/knees at right angles, proboscis crooked, the creature explored Alexander's hands, his wrists, the newgrown lawn of peach fuzz upon his arm. Then the bug stalked onto my desk. Six prehensile feet crept up my pencil tip, antennae waved at me. I thanked Alexander for the fine assassin bug, insect-sat for an hour, while cycles of unfinished work—larvae, pupae, wet-winged thoughts—buzzed in my head, gestated on my desk, flew out the window. Only later I read that assassin bugs can sting. This one didn't.

A fortnight in an unfinished and unscreened house on St. Thomas, where every evening the extensive collection of moths on the ceilings was different and always amazing, almost prepared me for Malaysia.

There are two hundred species of dragonflies on the Malay Peninsula, my 1956 *Encyclopædia Britannica* informed me, at least nine hundred species of lepidoptera and insects "diverse beyond computation of which many groups are imperfectly known." I computed and knew, imperfectly but intimately, many in the course of three hundred sixty-two humid days and nights scented with jasmine, curry, and fish in the east-coast village of Sungai Karang (meaning "river of shells") on Peninsular Malaysia's east coast. House lizards, called *chi-cheks*, were kept busy catching bugs.

So were our chickens, who often slipped in the kitchen door in search of bugs and crumbs. The rooster, auburn and bronze, stalked through the front door, followed by the black hen who frequently laid a speckled egg on my pillow. Iridescent emerald beetles the size of plums daunted or thrilled the chickens and lizards, as did the brown millipedes (disconcerting but harmless) and the red centipedes (deservedly infamous) who scuttled under the inch-high cracks between doors and floors.

While interesting to observe, neither insects nor chickens fulfilled me emotionally. I loved Malaysia, yet it was also a frequently lonely year, during which I watched a marriage, which for twenty-three years had had many good moments, peter out. But I learned to speak Malay, met other writers though they lived elsewhere around the country, and wrote—more about insects and chickens, than political and marital sadness. We had no phone, and mail crossed the Pacific as if by sea turtle and the jungles by white-handed gibbons, so I welcomed the rare morning when the village postman steamed up the rutted road on his red motorcycle with a letter.

The loneliness was mitigated by travels abroad both to give lectures and poetry readings and by less literary, more earthy, expeditions into the Malaysian jungles. Alexander, then thirteen, was a wonderful traveling companion, along with his Malay pal, Wan.

We ascended the brown river by long wooden canoe, hiked steep paths, camped a week in a hut in a clearing. By night it was ringed with glowworms, and large Cecropia-like moths came to our candles. At dawn we found prints of a tiger. Dawn also brought hordes of fat furry wasps with orange cummerbunds. Each day more of them got the message, swarmed to our sun-lit clearing, and mistook the flowers on my sarong for real. I switched to plain beige clothes and fled to the shady trails the wasps ignored.

But I don't remember one cockroach in Malaysia. Until Penang.

Alexander and I traveled all day by rickety inter-city taxi from Sungai Karang west across the Malay Peninsula, north by over-night train, west by ferry to the island of Penang, and in all directions by pedicab until we found an airy two-dollar-a-night hotel. The room was large and bare, with two clean beds and a welcome overhead fan. The washroom was across the wide central hall. The hall had a table and two chairs. After a day of exploring the island, inhabited mostly by Chinese Malaysians, and a supper of sea cucumbers, shark fins, and noodles, Alexander soon fell asleep. The other hotel guests also turned in early. I sat at that unsteady hall table half the night writing.

But I was not alone for long.

The cockroach hovered like a lend-lease dirigible, landed on a crack in the wall, then slowly walked down the wall and soon appeared on the other chair. Five inches long plus extensive feelers. All evening he sat (or stood) beside me, six feet (or hands) poised to scurry elsewhere. Since cockroaches predate vertebrates and would outlive humans, I could not begrudge him a seven-inch span of space, and shared time and light from the kerosene lamp.

Furthermore, I admired his ability to decamp: when threatened, run; survive in a crack; be patient; hide from the searchlight of sun, and then later, resume your station.

As he did the following nights as well, keeping me under observation or merely keeping me company. And so, in addition to some scientific interest, in time I felt a sort of gratitude.

Hand's Span
Frances Burton

We were allowed into the large, outdoor cages at the Centre. Inside I could sit quietly and watch. The monkeys would use me as an object to climb on; a fuzzy, hairy thing to clean their hands on. Whatever I was to them, I was not inimical. We had much in common: fingers that move, sneezing, pouchy places in the face that can contain food. These, on me, the mangabey named Matthew regularly inspected. Striding up to the seated me, or plopping down on top of me, with cool fingers and surprising gentleness, he pried open my lips and levered open my teeth to probe delicately in the space which should hold some slightly macerated fruit or plant part. His disappointment registered: with quicker jabs he probed again. Surely so rounded a structure must be full. Frustrated, he left, but I was enthralled. Not only had the monkey made contact with me, he had done so in terms familiar to him; there was, therefore, not only an acceptance of sorts, but a categorization of me as something familiar, and more than that: similar. But faces are readily seen; what of structures whose resemblance is transformed? The shod foot is a meaningless appendage. Matthew finds baring it a fascinating process. He watches; pulls on laces, mouths rubber and canvas, sniffs at socks. Toes. The fiveness is investigated. His hand riffles the digits and plucks each one, twisting, pulling, riffling again. The similarity stops where mobility and function end. My toes cannot return the touching, grabbing motion. The shape to which they are attached, inflexible, cannot respond to his gestures. He rushes off, returns to leap upon a shoulder and groom the more responsive hair. Sometimes I dare to peek into his brown eyes with their lustrous lashes. This he tolerates a fragile moment before he must turn away. But in that instant, it is as if. The illusion is probably mine. The cage adds to the impression that he comes to me. Where else could he have gone? I as novelty certainly have more significance than I as transformed monkey. The limitations of our contact seem clear.

Later and elsewhere, amongst monkeys that range freely within the purview and constraints of human regulation, there is more spontaneity to the exchange. These are *Macaca sylvanus* on Gibraltar. I have come to study two groups whose circumstances are unusual amongst primates: they roam quite freely on the peninsula inhabited also by twenty-five thousand people. No one really knows how long monkeys have been in that little space, two and one-half miles long by three-quarters of a mile wide, but I can track them back at least two centuries. Legend takes over where historical documents are missing, and the protection of the British Colonial Government extends to these animals because of their legendary role in saving this outpost, and thus the Empire, from invasion. There may be truth to this tale: macaques give warning barks when they are disturbed, which would certainly awaken sleeping sentries, and foil a sneak attack. But it is how the Gibraltarians feel about this mythopoeic event that is important. They revel in it. The idea that these pests, mischief makers, clowns could have saved an empire is humorous, touching, incredible, aggrandizing: the image of Gibraltar expands; the history of the settlement is enhanced; the significance of the colony is assured. The ambivalence the people feel towards the animals is resolved in favor of the monkeys.

Perhaps the monkeys have lived here with people since forever; perhaps the monkeys preceded the people by thousands of years—Gibraltar being a refuge habitat for what remains of a circum-mediterranean distribution of the species ancestral to all macaques. Their numbers are diminished now and directly reflect the vicissitudes of human existence. As the human population has grown, the competition for land space has become acute and the solution has been to curtail the size of the monkey population. Warfare has played a part, whether through stressing the population or more directly. The number of monkeys during the period of World War II fell so low that only importations from Morocco saved the population. The decision to bring in monkeys is said to have come from no less a personage than Winston

Churchill, who, recognizing the morale value of such an act for Great Britain as well as locally in Gibraltar, issued the order. Initially held in cages, where many of the imported monkeys succumbed to a variety of illnesses, the survivors were finally freed and allowed to roam the upper parts of "the Rock." Ultimately two groups were formed, separated by a quarter of a mile. One group met people daily and became a regular attraction both for the Gibraltarians and for the increasing number of tourists. The other group remained on military property which, until that land was transferred to civilian authority twenty years ago, could be visited with permission only.

What a marvel to sit near a monkey-made path, beneath the trees where the monkeys rested—acknowledged by them, known to them, ignored by them. When I am allowed to share the quiet as intense as meditation, insights come. More accurate, moments of awareness come of what was happening in monkey terms. Earlier, doing fieldwork in Africa, I had tried to start with accepted theory and fit behaviors to that constraint. In Gibraltar it became apparent that it was appropriate to listen and watch and first describe, waiting for knowledge before theorizing.

Wilma is old, nearly twenty. Her aged face is overhung with brows so heavy they block her vision, and like a person wearing bifocals, she tilts her head backward to gain a clear view. She occupies a curious position. She is the last to eat, the last to get a sunny spot, is always a distance from the others, is easily supplanted if there is some "goody" some other monkey wants. But she is SOMEBODY in the group in ways more subtle than contemporary theory can accommodate. Everyone in the group, particularly the young, attend to her every move. They monitor her vocalizations and gestures as they do no one else's, and they imitate her. If Wilma gives a warning bark, everyone looks where she directs; if the group is heading up the hill but Wilma lies down facing the opposite direction, the group will return and wait for her to move. And Wilma is a proven mother. For ten years and more she has birthed viable offspring who have come to take their places in the group. Perhaps her wisdom gives her her place within this group; she has watched the transition of her range from restricted land to public park and has learned to discriminate between those who would leave her be and those who would torment her. She sits by me. She is lush with the oil from eating olives too small to be of human use, from eating blade and leaf and flower and seed and the odd insect. The perfume of her fur is elusive—hard to catch and hold on to, but powerful when it drifts to me. I am overwhelmed by sun and scent and the warmth and the pressure of her flank touching mine. I do not move. Perhaps I do not breathe. The preciousness of this moment restrains me as much as the surety that a quick move would alarm her, perhaps resulting in injury to me. We look together towards the sea. My hair, her fur, blown by breezes reaching up the hillside: we sit like this for some time. Do we share in contemplation? (I would like to think so.) And then she leaves, the aged and roughened skin on her feet and bum make scuffling sounds as she moves off. Later that summer she gives birth to a female. Custom decrees that the Governor choose a name from amongst those who have contributed in some way to the Colony. The human is honored by connection to the monkeys because of the legend of how they saved the Empire. There is whimsy in this too; and ambiguity in having a monkey for a namesake.

Wilma is the most practiced of mothers. Her confidence makes her casual. Her experience gives her sure knowledge. The infant is raised unrestrained, undisciplined. Wilma brings Rosemary to me. I proffer seeds, which Wilma takes, her moist lips bending directly to the hand now held in hers, Rosemary at her belly. My extended hand is close to the infant's head, and she, perhaps not distinguishing digit from teat, grasps my little finger and begins to suck. Her gums are roughened by teeth forming beneath their surface. Her tongue works on the digit to extract what should be there. Wilma sees and ignores. I stay in that cramped position, unaware that I am cramped, unaware that I have not moved, totally concentrated on Wilma eating from my hand, feeling Rosemary suck my finger. I am no threat to them.

Nor to Mark, the male leader. He too has reached his second decade. He is scarred, one finger permanently distended from an old break, nearly toothless. His upper incisors are gone and he too has hugely overhanging brows that block his seeing. He deigns to play with the younger males. They do a kind of football ritual, bopping each other's shoulders but with no force, lest the gesture be misinterpreted. Shorter at the shoulder than most

adult males, Mark seems to have put his strength into his male-
ness, growing robust rather than tall, heavily muscled and empha-
tic in the genitalia. He is formidable. He is graceful for all his
bulk, and swift despite his age. That he commands respect is
apparent from the quick response his gestures get. He needs
merely to look at another individual for that one to cower, or
run, or stop what s/he is doing. I am impressed. I also see that
because he is wise and experienced, he can afford to receive
instruction from the young males—because he is old, perhaps
he also needs to. A dog comes into their range; the adolescent
males grunt; a juvenile gives the warning bark—Mark does not
react. Is this because he knows the dog; knows dogs; knows there
is no real danger? The adolescents intensify their gestures; one
rushes towards Mark grunting. Mark turns slowly and ambles
towards the dog, grabs it at the hips and flings it. The dog flees.

In the tradition of adult males on Gibraltar, Mark is allowed
to hold Rosemary. From the first day of her life he carries her
almost incessantly, until the next youngster is born. When Mark
is around, I am not worried about the other monkeys. Even
when an infant with an anxious mother or babysitter nearby
strays towards me, despite the threat, I do not worry. Mark will
intercept the young one, or threaten it away. When Mark sits by
me, he holds my arm. The power of his grip surprises me. I am
not hurt, nor does that seem to be his intent. He sits by me,
holding me with both hands and sometimes an odd foot. He
too is perfumed, muskier than Wilma but with that same ephem-
eral delicacy. I relish this contact. I do not seek it—I do not wish
to intrude—but I accept it as a gift. I accept this as an acceptance;
as permission to know more, to enter into an alien domain.
Once, I tease Mark. I cannot resist. He is sitting on top of my
tiny rented car, his leg dangling so that his foot is just above the
window. Slowly, without a sound, I lower the window and reach
my hand out to tickle his foot. It is coarse and toughened and
he reacts to this unexpected sensation with a start that makes
me giggle. He cannot respond; his senses lack *this* humor.

Mark bites an official at the prison which is located within his
group's range. He is shot. I am not forewarned; I cannot intervene. When I find out, it is too late. They say it is because he is
old anyway. A sharpshooter from the army was called in. One

bullet. Mark never heard the noise they tell me. I am not permitted to see him because of the blood. But I am offered the death bullet. I am guarded from the sight of blood but not from seeing the agent of the death which made the blood. This shift in values is hard for me.

The loss of Mark has repercussions. The male who takes over is young, lacks majesty. Disorder follows; sub-adult males are badly injured—one gets a broken arm and has to be put down—females are attacked. In time Ben secures his position; change continues. It is a dynamic system, this monkey troop: change is the only constant. Wilma dies and is not quite replaced by Rosemary. Wilma's sister Bridget dies and all the others I first knew go, are gone, are replaced or not quite by offspring. And I attend these events, noting, recording patterns and non-patterns.

I am honored with a namesake who grows to maturity and whom I witness involved in political events. One winter in the early 1980s, four young males left their natal troop high up on the Rock, where I had known Wilma and Mark and Ben, and went to the other group. Within the first few days of their arrival, they engaged one of the two incumbent adult males, Jimmy, in a dreadful fight. Under attack from front and behind, he must have lost track of where he was. The fight took him to the edge of a cliff from which he fell or was thrown to his death. Our autopsy of him indicated that he had broken his neck along the cliff wall before he hit the bottom. Jimmy had been in his prime. He had shared leadership of the group for over ten years with an old male called Sam. How sensible was their division of leadership and without serious competition: Jimmy predominated when the group was "in the bush," Sam when they were among people. Both bred and neither was the exclusive partner of any female, although friendships and persevering relationships were obvious. One of the four young intruders, Jake, made a play to stay in this group. He was wary of Sam, but did not challenge him. My namesake was the means by which Jake became integrated. Wherever Jake went, Frances followed. She pursued him relentlessly, posturing for him to groom her whenever he stopped moving. The more he did so, the more he relaxed; the more she reciprocated, the more that bond was reinforced. Grooming, and remaining with him, she gradually led him closer to the group. Within a couple of weeks, Jake came face to face with Sam. Only a few feet separated them. Frances went and groomed Sam, then returned and groomed Jake. She continued bridging and Jake came closer. Sam appeared tense, but unperturbed. The distance closed; Frances continued grooming each male alternately until only her body separated them. She had succeeded in bringing the stranger, the intruder, within a hand span's distance from the old male. Then she left. The two males looked at each other, and Jake began to groom Sam. For the time being, at least, Jake could stay.

This was my last visit to Gibraltar. Other researchers were coming in with paradigms that neatly identified every activity; predicted every move; obscured the complexity and texture in favor of the paradigm. It was time to move on, to see if my description of social process which I had learned in two small groups, each with only seventeen individuals, applied to larger groups. The theme of urban monkeys, of animals ranging freely within a context of human constraints, was not unique to Gibraltar. There is another British colony where macaques live, also a peninsula, but with a vastly larger human population—six million—and a very different cultural framework: Kowloon, the mainland side of Hong Kong. It seemed a propitious move.

Safer Sex for Salmon: The Spawning Channel

An Interview with Susan Maurer

Beth Bosk

It was in the course of my interview with Freeman House—who introduced the concept of salmon as "totem species of the Pacific Rim" into the bioregional glossary, and who now, as he has for many years, works at watershed restoration, among many other tasks, engaging in a kind of in vitro salmon spawning near the mouth of the Mattole—that I understood the depth to which, even among mutually admiring friends, our perceptions are gender-clouded.

As I listened to Freeman talk of the work, it occurred to me that what the men at the low-tech, hand-built hatchbox at Mill Creek were really doing was killing the female salmon—slitting open their bellies to collect their eggs—but only massaging the gonads of male salmon to squirt out the semen to fertilize the eggs and afterward setting them free. And as the male salmon continued their reproductory voyage upriver to spawn again, "on the natch," the men surely felt at least a modicum of vicarious pleasure.

I remarked (surprising both Freeman and myself with the language), "Egads, Freeman, this is gender terrorism! You're slaughtering females as a reproductive strategy? I'll bet there aren't any women doing this with you. There's got to be another way!"

About a week after the interview was published, I sat down at a table in the Mendocino bakery, and Nat Bingham, a salmon fisherman, leaned over to tell me that it bothered even him that the hatcheries killed salmon as the first step in artificial spawning. "There is a nonviolent spawning technique," he added. "And you guessed right. The person who is doing it is a woman."

Nat told me of the lone woman up past the Trinities, working on the north slope where she gets sun for only a short time each day, who was using an artificial channel. She was getting very good (just as good as anyone else's) results, but Fish and Game wanted to dump the project because her fry weren't going through their starting gates.

64

Before the week was out, I was sitting with Susan Maurer in her cabin, talking the way women talk science, talking out our musings. Science is there for any of us to recapture—as appropriate for coffee cup conversation as the problems with a lover. You can chat Gaian precepts the way you tell tales of your children. And the real fact is, one has to uncover women like Susan Maurer—who, whether they are uncovered or not, tenaciously do the real work.

SUSAN MAURER: Eight years ago I came here to the base of the Marble Mountains Wilderness Area. The watershed starts high in the mountains that divide the Trinities from the Marbles. Our watershed, the Scott River watershed, flows through an agricultural valley before it comes down into the canyon where I live and work. Then it's another hundred miles—measuring in a straight line—to the ocean. The fish that come all the way up here have quite a journey, a lot more obstacles to overcome than those that spawn in coastal streams. There's commercial fishing at the mouth of the Klamath and Indian gill-net fishing. There're natural obstacles, waterfalls, changes in river courses, sedimentation from logging. There is also fishing by sportsmen.

Then, if they finally get up to their spawning areas, often there is not enough water, because a lot of it is diverted for agricultural purposes, so they'll have to hole up in pools and wait. Hopefully, before they get ripe, there is enough water so they can get up.

Are you saying that built into the salmon is a waiting mechanism, something that allows the females to suppress the maturation of their eggs?

SUSAN: I don't really know if when it's time to spawn they can control that to any degree. I don't think we know much at all about fish. We're learning some things, but we always apply our perspective to them. They live in a different world—not totally different—but different from ours.

I can tell you what I observe here, below the bridge you came over, where there is water coming over but not enough for them to make their jump. If the fish are getting close to spawning time, but they are not ripe, they stay in a pool and face upstream. Those that are ready to spawn are trying to find places to spawn, and they are very territorial. The males are running off the other males and the females are running off the females. If they have been able to select a redd site—a place where they are going to dig their nest—there's a lot of action, a lot of spinning around.

The female goes on her side and she moves gravel. She digs a pit. She's selected the site because it has a good-sized gravel, between two inches to, they say, six inches for large salmon, but the salmon of the Scott River use only three-inch gravel. They dig down a pit almost a foot with their tail and deposit the eggs. One redd is usually about four to five feet in diameter, if it were circular. It's usually more oblong, and in the wild it's going to be even more longish because it's not perfect gravel.

And then she'll spend her final days just sort of tending this. She rolls on her side and flips her tail and fans this gravel, keeping off sediment and debris and flushing water through. She's trying to get the eggs to have as much oxidation as possible.

That, of course, is the main problem in wild habitat now—that siltation occurs because of erosion that results from logging or road building or other impacts on the land. All this washes down, covers the gravel, and suffocates the eggs.

Here at the spawning channel, the male is right there—there seems to be some kind of scent—when the female is actually spawning. There's a lot of courting going on. The male does a neat little shimmy right next to her. Sometimes you can see the cloud of sperm actually covering the eggs. Other times I don't observe that, and I don't know if it is because I don't see it or if he's not fertilizing at that time.

Once she deposits some eggs, she'll move upstream and backfill this. She'll dig another pit, and in the process of this, the gravel gets moved downstream by the speed of the water, covering the eggs she's deposited. She moves upstream gradually over the course of four or five days, depositing her eggs, because they don't all ripen at once, and this is something that when they spawn artificially is not taken into account—all the eggs are taken from a female at one time.

Ah, the homily "Don't put all your eggs in one basket" could have been written for salmon. And how perfect that the river itself pushes a protective blanket over the eggs. Is it any wonder Native traditions speak of rivers as "alive"? Here you have a creek brooding salmon eggs, much like a mother hen broods her eggs. Maybe "foster mothering" is the better concept, or perhaps this is all part of one complex mothering as with a Mother Earth.

SUSAN: This is an artificial channel, but what I observed here seems to be very classic spawning. The female will deposit some eggs, and then she'll be done for the evening—she tends to work in the evening—and after the male has fertilized the eggs, he will go off to find another female who is fresh. Meanwhile, she tends her redd. She is almost constantly working. Then she will seek a little quiet time very close to her redd.

This is much different from the males, who will go back down to a big pool at the bottom and fight amongst themselves until there is another female spawning.

Do they fight brutally, or is it primarily display?

SUSAN: I'd say mostly display though I've seen one male grab another by the tail and spin him around. I think they are determining who gets the prime female as each comes to prime, and that order gets established, it seems, during the daytime, during the time when the female isn't actually spawning.

Let me back up a bit: what we had in the spawning channel were twenty females and fifteen males that we brought in. They were trapped in the channel. The males mostly stayed in the bottom pool, and the females—not all twenty of them spawned at once, this took place over a month and a half—were spawning, half a dozen at one time, at selective sites. They'd spread themselves out. They'd gone through their territorial behavior, which adamantly says, "This is mine. Don't be messing with it," as they determined the area of their redd.

The males determine their order in the pool; and when the females start spawning activity, the dominant male—and he may not be the first to jump on up to where she's spawning, there may be a smaller male who is up there first—but it seems as soon as the female starts her spawning activity in earnest, the most dominant male booms right up there and chases off the other male.

In the hatchbox situation, sperm from several males are used to fertilize eggs squeezed out of one female all at one time. It sounds as if in your system one male is doing all the fertilization. How do the other males fit in? Are they just there for the dominant male to match his mettle against?

SUSAN: What we observed in the spawning channel is that there were two males that probably serviced two-thirds of the females, and only one time did I observe one female with more than one male. All the other times, there was just one male who was with her.

There are also the little jacks, two-year-old precocious males. They're able to fertilize eggs, and they sometimes can sneak in. They'll get in the shadow of the female where the dominant male doesn't see them and just boom!—there's a cloud of sperm.

What do you think is the survival value of precocious males coming upriver ahead of what we assume their time? Why do you think Nature worked it out that way?

SUSAN: For insurance. The fry from one year, when they go out to sea, will come back over a many year period of time. The earliest the males will come back will be as two-year-olds. The females come back as three-year-olds. But there are a good number of females and males that come back as four-year-olds, some as five-year-olds, some as six-year-olds. And that's in case there are any major catastrophes anywhere so that one whole class isn't lost.

Now, I'm not sure exactly what happens in the wild, but I would venture to say it's probably more likely that there is only one male with the females at any time. With a hatchbox situation, the thinking behind it says, "There is more diversity." But I'm not sure diversity is what Nature is reaching for in this situation. We don't know what advantages are lost to the next generation by not permitting the "fittest" male to prevail. Now, it might not be that at all. It might be that each male simply becomes the "fittest" somewhere down the line in time. One of the disadvantages of a closed channel is that we can't figure that out.

Tell me how the channel came about, and in more detail, how it is constructed.

SUSAN: First of all, you should know the project was conceived by a man, a fisheries biologist who works for the U.S. Forest

Service. His name is Jack West. Spawning channels are not brand new. There are spawning channels up in British Columbia. This particular type—from pictures I've seen of other ones—is smaller in scale, and Jack West's original design was a very harmonious type of system.

It was essentially to be just like a small stream, a diversion from a creek, Kelsey Creek, which is a tributary of the Scott River. It was going to be just like a little parallel creek to Kelsey Creek, with water from Kelsey Creek flowing through and back into Kelsey Creek.

You have to picture the channel as linear, six hundred feet long and twenty feet wide in a series of eleven steps. There is a weir, a little dam, at the end of each step, where flashboards can be put in to control the depth of the water. Also screens, for later rearing fry, to confine them.

Originally, it was going to be strictly a spawning channel, not a rearing facility. The idea was that the fish need a spawning habitat where they make decisions on their own. We already have hatcheries. We don't need another. However, there's quite a conflict between State Fish and Game and the federal agency. The state has jurisdiction over wildlife—the salmon—but the federal government owns the land in question. In order for this project to get approved, Jack had to comply with the specifications the State Department of Fish and Game had outlined, and it had to be a rearing facility. . . . There were other stipulations. [*sighs*] It had to have a fence around it, a bear-proof fence. Of course, if a serious bear decided to come through, it would have no problem getting in.

The whole design had to be altered. When salmon hatch out, they are very small. It's hard to get something fish-tight, especially when you are talking about rip-rap rock sides. So this whole thing had to be plastic-lined, which wasn't in the original plan. And then we had to get bird netting to put over the top to keep the birds from eating the fry. It really just changed the whole concept of an as-natural-as-possible artificial stream.

What were the consequences of abiding by State requirements and elaborations?—I know there had to be consequences.

SUSAN: The bird net was to prevent primarily kingfishers, herons, possibly some osprey from getting to the fry. Kingfishers probably could have done some damage. We killed two kingfishers because they got caught in the net. And the fence killed a kestrel that ran into it and broke its wing.

There was no shading from trees, no cover. During the spawning time, a friend, who was helping me with this as a friend, not an employee, and I cut boughs and braced them with the rock rip-rap so that they hung out over the water's edge, so that from a fish's point of view, there was quite a bit of cover. And it was amazing. The fish used it immediately. The first two weeks we had the fish in there we didn't do that because we were still abiding by the book, but I think it had something to do with the success in spawning, because the fish, when people would come, would naturally get under these shaded areas.

The fish spawned beautifully. From the spawning-channel standpoint, it was a success, as much as you can say after one year. But incubation in Kelsey Creek is long—that's totally a function of the water temperature. Kelsey Creek is a very cold creek. We're much higher than the coastal streams. We obviously have snow melt, and that's what keeps things so cold here.

That distressed the Department of Fish and Game, and the project was criticized because the incubation period was so long. The fish finally hatched out in May. In a hatchbox situation or in a hatchery, the incubation period is much shorter.

And then Fish and Game required that these fish be raised to yearling size. Their thinking is that the survival rate is much greater when they are released at yearling size, but this is not what happens in this stream naturally.

What happens naturally?

SUSAN: The fish here move out as the water starts dropping off early in the summer. In rearing these fish, we have to artificially feed them; we give them this commercially prepared fish food, primarily composed of brine shrimp, which is what they would find in an estuary, but who knows what else is in it to preserve it and what is left out? Another thing that comes to mind is that by rearing these fish, they haven't learned natural hunting techniques. You get this large-sized fish that is used to feeding at regular intervals, and all of a sudden it gets released. I think it's missing the information it would have learned as a young fish on how to survive out there. Fish and Game says their survival is greater, but I have some doubts on the trade-off.

One of the reasons I felt we did not need to operate Kelsey Creek channel with a rearing phase is because Kelsey Creek and the channel are very rich in aquatic insect life. We don't have anything quantitative yet, but just through observation, during the season I was down there, the mayflies, the stoneflies, both the hatches that occur and the nymphs that are in the water, are incredibly rich, and that food source must be better than the artificial pellets.

I think that is something that needs to be looked at—especially if other spawning channels are going to be built, which is the intent of the Forest Service. We should study very closely how efficient nature is—what the natural carrying capacity is without having to feed the fish artificially.

How did you get involved in the spawning channel?

SUSAN: Living right here, I watched the construction—there was mostly floodplain and gravel bars on the site, but they took out a few trees—and I inquired how it was going to be operated. I heard it was going out on contract, so I wrote a proposal, which was accepted, and I went to work.

My work, really, was just sort of to be there. During the spawning, from mid-October to mid-December, I was there twenty-four hours a day. Then, during the winter, I came daily to check the temperature and clean the dams and screens after storms—sometimes I had to break the ice to get at them. I spent a lot of time in my lounge chair with polarized glasses and my notebook. I kept a journal and tried to note everything I possibly could. I also monitored water temperature, air temperature, rainfall. I did some water quality tests, like dissolved oxygen, conductivity.

There must have been a Jane Goodall kind of excitement about this for you.

SUSAN: Each fish seemed to have a different personality. I don't know how else to describe that. I particularly keyed into the females because of their association with a redd—I knew the fish that was in this particular spot was going to be the same fish time after time. And I could fix on certain markings. Even as she started deteriorating, I could still retain the impression of who she was.

I named some because of their markings. Often salmon will have lamprey marks on them. A lamprey is another anadromous species, often called eels. They have big suction lips and they catch a ride on the salmon. There would be lamprey marks on the side of the fish in specific places. You could tell a fish by that.

Some were identifiable because of their distinct coloring. Some were more dark-olive color, and some of them were more silvery. And they were different sizes. Some were just much more aggressive. There were those females, if I was another female swimming by her redd, I'd go by fast because she'd really let you know. One in particular, she didn't want any other female in two-thirds of the whole section she was in.

Other fish were much more affiliative. They would spawn within three feet of each other and not seem to be too threatened. There would just be a little bit of exchange.

It wasn't only that the fish seemed to have different personalities, but they were also involved in separate subdramas that individuated them for me. Maybe if I read a couple of excerpts from my journal you'd get an idea of that.

October 6: Big Brown was behind the bubbles with only his head sticking out, viewing me. Geez, was he gnarly! His jaw was noticeably hooked and his color was a yellow-brown and he had various wounds on his side. He didn't look happy that I was in his space . . .

October 11: I took fins and got a better look at things. By crawling over the concrete on the north side of the weir, I managed to get in without disturbing the fish. Overall their appearance is one of decay. I got a great view as each one passed by one to two feet from my face—fish that are two to three feet long and weigh up to twenty-five pounds. The brightly colored red males look even more spectacular up close. One female's mouth is really falling apart on the left side. You can see the jaw and a hole into the mouth cavity.

The whole time the salmon come up into fresh water, they don't eat. They're living off the stored fats from their ocean feedings. As they use up that fat, then they start using their bodies to live off—their muscle tissue gets consumed next. They are actually living off their own bodies for months! It takes a good month and a half for those fish to get up to Kelsey Creek, and all that time, it is with no food. And then another month or two for the whole spawning routine. That's why the carcasses look so bad.

October 30: Another fish died this evening, another male with no nose. He was a first-batch male and still had a lot of sperm left in him. He got aced out by the Red Brothers. Two-Lampreys almost bit the dust by getting gilled in the grates before the boards were put back in. I rescued her and she swam up channel . . .

The female will tend her redd up to two weeks after she is done spawning, and you can see her deteriorating. But she still has this spirit in her, and to me, it's like *total life*. Then bamm! Overnight she just dies. She's there on her redd, and she stays there until her dying breath; then she floats down and gets washed up against the rocks. I would take the carcasses out and weigh them and measure their length and take a scale sample—that's a way of aging fish—and cut them open to see how many eggs were left in the female and if there were sperm left in the males.

You have the traditional experiences of the naturalist: you camp out near your subject, you begin to see their behavior personalized. But in the end you are just another scientific scavenger. How did it feel to you, retrieving the carcasses of fish you had come to know?

SUSAN: Because I watched them, I felt I was a little more than just the coon who had come down and found dinner. I didn't need their flesh for energy. Perhaps I got energy from just having them give me a chance to see what that part of their life is about. I suppose that could be scavenging energy.

But I always felt a lot of respect for them, and even though it was a smelly old dead fish carcass, I didn't want to just heave it over the bank. I'd place it down and there was always some recollection—remembering the last few weeks of its life, the part

I could see here in the channel—and there was always some good feelings about it. I did it with respect.

What happened to your project?

SUSAN: The eggs hatched out in the spring—very well—we figured the emergence was very, very successfu. More successful than you would find in the wild in this river at this particular time because we didn't have the siltation and we didn't have the predation either. There were no large fish that were allowed in there—generally a natural part of the food pyramid—and we had a bird net. I began feeding the fry the latter part of May—at that point I started working again all day every day—and fed them all through the summer. The feeding was required. That wasn't the part of the contract that I looked forward to. I believed it would be a better project without rearing them, especially after they first showed signs of smolting. During smolt, the salmon turn silvery, and their behavior totally changes. They want out. I don't know all the things that they sense, but one of the things has to do with the amount of water. When water starts dropping off, they must know that it is time to get out before they can't get out.

Did any get out?

SUSAN: It's very hard to estimate when you are talking forty or fifty thousand fish. We'd get in there with masks and snorkels and cameras, and take pictures, and we did some estimates by marking cubic meters in the channel and then trying to count the number of fish—a couple of hundred maybe, in a cubic meter. They'd stay still enough to count if we just drifted quietly in the water with them.

The first time we noticed there was a lot of strange movement was when about five thousand of them appeared in the settling pond. They had found a way under a log weir where the uppermost screen was, and they swam upstream through a culvert under a road and into the settling pond. They just did this overnight. Apparently they are tied into lunar cycles; they moved on a new moon. I figured, "That's all right." I'd feed them up there, then feed the rest of them down below. In the settling pond, they didn't have the same protections that had been required by Fish and Game, but they fared just as well. The fish that moved were the bigger ones.

And did they try also the leave that pond?

SUSAN: I think they were trying to get out of there, but at that point there was no way. So those fish stayed in the pond, and then we seined them out and brought them back down to the lower part with the intent of tagging them all with a coated wire nose tag, which at first sounded like a great idea to me. It's a way to quantify what we have, and being that it is a new project and we need *proof* of how successful it is, it seemed like a good way to do it.

In tagging, the fish are seined and fed into a trap, and from the trap they are again netted out and anesthetized with a drug called MS222. The technicians, mostly women, who are on contract with Fish and Game, can tag five or six thousand fish per day, per tagger. Fish and Game had four of them come up with the intent to tag about forty thousand fish.

They had everything tagged in a day and a half. We only had twelve thousand fish tagged, and there were no more fish. We said, "Hmmm, what happened? Where did they go?" It's purely speculation where they went. I think they found a hole.

That area where the channel was dug once had some cabins on it, and there was some piping left behind. The creek has changed its course many times. Possibly there could be a conduit under there that they found. They are amazing how they can go between cracks, and they could have just found a way that went from the channel to the creek. There's one main seep that we noticed in the creek that is coming from the channel, and I believe that is where they went out.

That afternoon after we tagged the last fish I was pretty distressed about the whole thing because, on that level, it indicated we only had twelve thousand fish emerge, which I knew was not the case. But I didn't have any way to prove it. I went snorkeling in the creek, and from that seep on down, I saw large, artificially fed salmon fry. I didn't find them upstream. There weren't that many in there, but I think that indicates that once they found a way out, they bolted. They probably got down to the estuary in a couple of weeks. [*laughs*] Which is really kind of fine.

What happened after the head count?

SUSAN: Right at the time of the tagging was when the fires broke out, and the whole ridge above Kelsey Creek was on fire. The day after tagging was the day cf the lightning burst. By the second day, you couldn't even see the end of the channel. And by the third day, I was packed for evacuation. I was real concerned about the fish that were left in the channel.

Because they were drugged with this MS222, they weren't supposed to be released for twenty-one days, and Fish and Game wouldn't authorize the release even with the fire threat. So these fish hung in there until late October.

Because the main belief is that the fish escaped underground, through the channel, through the plastic, that there were leaks in the system—and obviously, there are leaks in that kind of system; it was never really designed to rear fish—Fish and Game required that the Forest Service repair it, and they would not allow more adults to be brought in until it was repaired.

But the Forest Service couldn't repair it until the fry were released, because you have to drain it down. So the repairs did not get made in time for this year's run.

The real interesting part of that—which pleases me greatly, although it may ace me out of a job—is that once the ladder came up, it was the open system it was originally designed to be. And guess what happened? Two chinook pairs came up on their own and spawned, and probably more would have come, but because of low water, they couldn't make it up the ladder. Fifteen cojo salmon spawned in there, and steelhead also. All totally natural. There's no money out to hire someone. There's no bird net up. The fish have built redds in the channel. They just spread themselves out beautifully. So it's working even though it is not "operating." That's really the bottom line.

All of us who have ever been engaged in any kind of research involving other species know that the hard-hearted, lethal situations set up to keep an experimental situation so-called controlled are simply not necessary and often provide perverted and erroneous information. And the funders are never present to watch the consequences of forcing an animal into an unnatural act.

SUSAN: Even some of the rationale for doing the project in the first place got to me. One time, the Forest Service brought down the local Lions Club. The district ranger was giving the tour, and I just happened to overhear him telling this group of men that this type of channel could "replace"—and he used that word—five to ten miles of river habitat. I was appalled that this was the line the Forest Service, or at least this particular individual, was taking with men who are involved heavily in timber harvest. So they could think that when further degradation occurs, all they need to do is slop in a spawning channel and that takes care of the problem.

It doesn't. There are elements that are found in the wild that are not found in Kelsey Creek spawning channel. By boosting an edge, which seems to be the thrust of enhancement projects, we may be introducing some elements that nature has chosen to weed out ages ago because they are not effective.

We call salmon our "totem species." Or we call them an indicator species, their health and number an indicator of the health of an ecosystem. Listening to you describe the intricate digging and scouring spawning involves, are not female salmon engaged in a very specialized dredging operation that our river systems may need, perhaps even to flow, so that to selectively sacrifice female salmon in artificial spawning may have consequences beyond procreativity?

SUSAN: That's a good possibility. They certainly move and clean the gravel. I think there are so many little subtle things that are all a part of the whole interdependency required for this system to survive that that very well could be an important part. Perhaps they move some sort of aquatic insect in a certain stage of development. There are so many things that could be a part of their behavior that we don't even know.

One of the important things we must consider as restoration workers is taking a look at the entire watershed. We can have a small little facility here at Kelsey Creek, but that is not going to do much in the long run if we do not look at the whole setup: sedimentation that is coming down from the high reaches, water diversions.

There's another whole aspect that occurred while I was on contract. I am just down there, right, and I'm watching all these fish, and I think, "There's a lot here for people in this community to learn from." So I set up field trips with the schools.

Kids love fish. They are so intrigued. Here is something so tangible—also so different from other wildlife, because it is a totally different medium they live in. When I have field trips with children, we spend a lot of time not talking but just observing. We'll have the polarized glasses (those magic glasses) to look through that cut the glare, so they can see much better. And it's amazing. I don't even have to have a plan. They'll just start asking questions.

What I'm really fired up about now is the whole concept in education of Adopt-a-Watershed, where a school can adopt a small stream or a creek near the school site and get involved in survey work on it, rehab work—all of which can be tied into the science framework the state requires.

One thing that living in Siskiyou County has taught me is that stability comes with diversity: the more things you can do, the better off you are going to be.

During the fire we called this place Planet Kelsey because the smoke was so dense. I was working dispatch. I was on the radio from six p.m. to six a.m. and running the channel during the daytime. I hike these hills, and I know all the places that were burning up as word of them came in. And it made me realize how tenuous everything is. Things change all the time, and we are alive for such a short period of time, we don't see the kind of long-range changes that matter.

My guess was that when I found a nonviolent technique for human-intervened spawning, there would be a woman here doing the work.

SUSAN: The woman who is doing this spawning work is Mother Nature and not this woman. I'm just watching, and I find it beautiful, fascinating to watch. And I think it is an opportunity the fish are providing for our species, to get a little glimpse of what goes on in the wild that we don't usually see. People who fish may occasionally see a pair spawning. In the spawning channel where I sat for hours day after day, I could see more than just a pair who happened to be together in one spot. I could see the interactions, the labor involved. I felt it such a privilege to get that glimpse.

Among Wolves
Jean Pearson

T here were no real wolves in Bethlehem, when I was born in that Pennsylvania steel town. My first encounter with a wolf took place in the church social room where, one evening, all of us kids were treated to a puppet theater version of "Little Red Riding Hood." After the performance the puppeteer came down the aisle and tried to get me to shake hands with the Big, Bad Wolf—a ferociously grinning marionette whose clacking jaws grabbed at my wrist. I was very little, and I backed away from him in a hurry.

When I was four, I nearly died. A mysterious illness. It hurt to walk. I remember an endless succession of days and nights in a dim room in the hospital. My glands and bones ached. Against the doctors' advice, my parents took me home. Every day my mother fed me a broth made from marrow bones until the word "bone" became lodged at the very center of my consciousness. As I gradually regained strength, the wolf dreams began. Large ghost-like animals glided through my room at night and stood beside my bed like huge pale dogs. I never saw their teeth. Sometimes three of them would weave a silent, ghostly dance through the rooms of our house. One turned his head and stared me straight in the eye, and I sat up in bed, sweating with terror, and stared back at him till he turned his head away. Slowly, his image faded and I was alone in the dark, knowing I had been dreaming. The wolves' presence was double-edged—I feared them, yet I knew they protected me. They were graceful and powerful. I did not know what it was they guarded me for or from.

It is the summer of 1983. I attend a creative writing seminar at the Naropa Institute in Boulder, Colorado. The big attraction is

Gary Snyder's week-long series of talks on poetry and place. My dog, a large white Hungarian sheep dog, sits with me during the lectures in the Buddhist meditation room. The closest living creature to my dream wolves, Dogga came into my life at a critical juncture and remains my inseparable companion. Snyder welcomes both of us to his class. His words and ideas resonate deeply: to dwell mindfully on earth we must know well the region of our birth, become one with the land, rediscover its prehistory and the spirit of the people who lived there before us. When I return to Bethlehem, I read everything I can find about the Lenni Lenape, or Delaware Indians, the first people to live in what is now the Lehigh Valley. I learn that the Minsi clan of the Lenni Lenape regularly crossed the river not far from my home. The clan's totem animal was the wolf.

The wolves were waiting for me in the deepest part of my life. Now they lead me underneath Bethlehem into a deeper, more primal connection with the land than any I have been taught by the colonizing, civilized, westernized world. For the first time, I know how to make use of my childhood wolf-visions. I follow the wolves back through time to a sense of what this place was before European culture drained it of its wildness. I begin to feel like one of the first people, a hunter-gatherer learning from the earth. When I walk along the Monocacy Creek with Dogga, a totally different paradigm of how the universe works springs up around me. I step into prehistory. The red-tailed hawk and the white heron descend to give me direction. Even the Lenape name of the creek—Monakessi, "stream with several large bends"—gives direction. My own white wolf walks with me. From William "Sauts" Bock, spiritual leader of the Lenape Wolf Clan, I learn that if a wolf crosses your path, he gives you long life.

How maligned nature and animals have been! Every original, primal, wild, self-willed life that resists the "civilized" world's obsession with its own exploitative order becomes for me an indication of freedom and sanity. Saving ourselves from excess civilization is the critical issue of my generation. The wolves, among the planet's most adaptable large mammals, are faced with the very real possibility of extinction in the wild before the end of this century. In all of the contiguous United States *and* Alaska, fewer than eight thousand remain. And it is humans who have nearly driven their species to death. We must not allow the extinction of wolves!

December 13, 1984: I wake in the middle of the night and know I must use my imagination to help the wolves. I will gather all the material I can find that portrays their beauty, intelligence, courage, and social nature. I will find the stories, legends, and poetry to once and for all lay to rest the myth of the "Big, Bad Wolf." As I gather tales at the Museum of the American Indian Library, as poems and stories pour in from across the country, I am increasingly aware that I walk in the thin air of my own ideal images of wolves. I need to experience them first-hand, observe real wolves and bodily interact with them. There are several sanctuaries in the United States where such work is possible: Wolf Haven in Tenino, Washington; the Wild Canid Survival and Research Center in Eureka, Missouri; and Wolf Park, a wildlife sanctuary in Battle Ground, Indiana, where students can observe wolves in semi-natural conditions.

September, 1986: Three years after Gary Snyder's lectures have put me on the path toward reclaiming wildness, my dog and I drive through the warm Indiana night. We are on our way to the wolves. I have signed up to take Wolf Park's four-week practicum in wolf ethology, and Dogga has special permission to attend, too. After phoning ahead to park director Erich Klinghammer that we'll be arriving late, we drive through the open gate at eleven p.m. As we pull around the circular driveway, Suzanne Klinghammer is waiting for us. Wolf Woods, the one-acre enclosure where the pack of eleven wolves lives, is illuminated at full power. A half-inflated volley ball comes tumbling toward us out of the night and behind it, Erich Klinghammer, calling out something between a challenge and a greeting. I introduce my dog to him, and he introduces us to the wolves. Seven pairs of gleaming, hungry eyes fix intently on us from behind the high chain link fence. For the first time in my life I watch my dog, whose sheep-guarding ancestors were bred strong enough to ward off wolves, avert her gaze. She doesn't wish to provoke a pack of natural enemies. She knows her best response is to avoid their challenging stare. We are shown to our quarters at the Visitors' Center where we will live for the next month. Gale Motter, the live-in assistant, welcomes Dogga and me warmly. It's easy to see she loves animals—not a bone of species-superiority in her body! It will be good to share living space with this human.

Every Saturday morning at Wolf Park, the regular volunteers are on cleanup duty. Armed with aluminum pails and a pair of tongs, they scour the acre of brushy ground hunting for wolf scat. The reward for this labor is the chance to socialize with the pack. The moment has come for me to meet the wolves in a "hands-on" encounter. With a thrill of apprehension and excitement, I enter the enclosure behind Gale and Pat Goodman, the park's assistant director. Four wolves run toward me eagerly and, though I know I should stretch out my hands to them in a confident gesture of welcome, instinct jams my closed fists deep into the pockets of my vest. Instantly, two wolves stand on either side of me and seize my flannel shirt cuffs and tug hard, trying to unearth the secrets hidden in my pockets. I open my palms and show them nothing. Fortunately, Pat is there to distract the wolves from me and relieve the pressure I feel from being ganged up on. I find it difficult to lean over them the way Pat and Gale and full-time volunteer Don Bailey do, giving them exuberant words of praise and stroking their fur. Though that is clearly what these wolves want and expect, I am afraid. But as I stand in this mingling of humans and wild dogs, a joyous surge of belonging rises in my throat and face, and I reach out to caress the harsh gray fur on the back and flank closest to me.

I don't yet know them by name. They are simply "the wolves" to me, not yet distinct individuals. In my room at the Visitors' Center, I study the Wolf Identification Chart. If the wolf is black, then it's Mephisto. That one should be easy. If the wolf is slender with a long muzzle and long body and a cape-like marking on her back, then it's Lailah. Hmm! Faust is charcoal-gray with a black stripe down his muzzle. Imbo has a long bushy tail. The pale tan male, the only wolf in this pack not hand-raised by humans, is Ohtsu. The dark brown female is Kaleah. Kesho (pseudonym "Piglet") is short, fat, and aggressive. Yes, I remember seeing that wolf. He reminds me of a former German professor. If the corners of the wolf's mouth look as if he'd eaten licorice, that's Akili. Eleven wolves in the pack. Who's missing? Naima, with a dark cape-like marking across her back. Lailah, Kaleah, Naima—it will be hardest to tell those three young females apart. And then the pack's grand old sire and dam: dignified Tornado, the twelve-year-old alpha male, and elegant Venus, almost white, the alpha female.

Wolves are highly social animals, highly intelligent and well suited for group living. But the crowding and pressures of captivity, even the semi-captivity of Wolf Park, result in extremes of social display, more frequent dominance struggles than would normally occur in the greater space and freedom of life in the wild. Here, confined to one acre, the wolves cannot easily avoid each other and tensions mount quickly. In the wild, as in captivity, a strong sense of hierarchy prevails in the pack, with the leading male and female pair referred to as the alpha wolves. The hierarchy of the wolf pack is structured according to age and a subtle range of interactive and fighting skills, not sex, with the older animals of both sexes usually ranking above the younger. As Barry Lopez points out in his compelling book *Of Wolves and Men*, the image of a wolf pack dominated by a male leader is more the wish-image of an overly masculinized human culture than it is the rule among wolves. In those rare cases where a pack is led by a single wolf rather than a pair, the alpha animal may be female or male. Because in the wild the female chooses the denning site where her pups will be born, her decision always determines where the pack will hunt during the weeks following the birth of a litter. As they grow to maturity, young females match their male litter mates in speed and hunting skill.

Achieving alpha status is usually the result of repeated fights and assertions of power through the ranks of both sexes. Remaining in alpha position often has more to do with skill at avoiding conflict and maintaining a viable harmony within the pack. This quality is certainly prominent in Tornado. Well past his physical prime, he has held on to the position of lead male through his social skill. He never insists on eating first, and his dominance displays are directed at low-ranking wolves, letting the serious contenders for his own alpha status—Kesho, Akili, and Imbo— battle it out among themselves. Among the females, sovereign Venus often reclines on a raised platform, projecting an air of calm self-assurance as she impassively regards the squabbles of the younger wolves. There is no one to match her. For the past six years, she has been the dominant female—the first to give birth to pups each spring. When wolves mate they are literally bound together by their sexual organs for as long as thirty minutes. This brief but inescapable physical bond may in some way explain why wolves in the wild are unusually loyal mates and good parents, both father and mother caring for and raising their young.

I stand outside Wolf Woods, peering through the fence at the wolves, going over the chart in my hand. They all look so alike! The first wolf I recognize—really recognize as an individual—is Kaleah. It is she who first comes joyously dancing to the fence whenever I walk by. After several such conspicuous welcomes, what choice do I have but to dance a greeting in return? In her open, gold eyes, charm and affection have completely replaced the cold gleam I saw that first night. She directs her whole personality toward me whenever she sees me, and soon I can distinguish her from the others, even at a distance. Once this happens, the identities of the other wolves quickly fall into place. But it was that graceful young wolf, the lowest-ranking female, who made the first overture of acceptance toward me, who first let me look into a wolf's soul.

A flurry of wolves in sunlight races along the fence as my dog trots proudly down the road. By now there is a curiosity between cousins, and my dog has overcome her initial intimidation. With seventy-five acres of alfalfa field, pond, and pasture to dig in, she is just as enamored of Wolf Park as I am. Dogga follows along when I go to talk with the wolves and, with any luck, to record their howls. I use a segment of howls recorded on the previous night to induce another round. In the night, I wake to the mournful and comforting polyphony of wolf voices. It rises up over my roof and across the world. In one of his poems, William Stafford calls the sound of howling wolves "that band of sorrow . . . that long pang across the horizon . . . a banner of woe." Yes, it sounds that way, yet it is also deeply consoling, like any nakedly honest, heartfelt utterance.

At the end of my first week at Wolf Park, Gale and Pat take me to the shed where they butcher dead animals for the wolves—road-killed deer, a dead calf we have hauled from a neighbor's dark barn the night before. They ask if I will help them quarter an animal. No, I can't stomach the thought. I haven't eaten a mammal in three years. I will feed the animal parts to the wolves, heaving a hindquarter or a forequarter over the chain link fence. But I won't dismember the body. Yet another refusal: I find it too difficult to throw a severed head in to the wolves. I am reminded of a biography of Anne Boleyn I read in high school—the scene in which Thomas More's brave daughter sails down the Thames at midnight to pluck her father's head from a spike on Tower Bridge. Henry VIII had a taste for beheadings, as a grim warning to his subjects not to thwart *their* alpha's brutal power-hunger. Why do we use the word "brutal"—like the brutes—to describe the cruelty inherent in our own species? I know that anything wolves might do to another creature is less cruel than what humans have done to their own and every other species throughout most of history.

The next day, I watch with fascination and not a trace of horror as the wolves tear into the carcass of the calf. Wolves need meat to live and it isn't easy to find enough on Indiana highways to feed a pack of wolves. When there's a shortage of road-killed animals, the wolves are generally fed zoo food. But today it's fresh food. To get the calf's carcass into the enclosure, the wolves are first lured through a sliding wood door into a separate section of Wolf Woods. Then the carcass is brought in and chained to a tree, and the wolves are let loose on it. Several wolves attack the "kill" at once, then Kesho makes a snarling display of dominance. He rips into the calf's abdomen with his teeth, raising his bloody muzzle and baring his fangs. The other wolves back off. Imbo calmly climbs onto one of the resting platforms, stretches his paws neatly in front of him, and watches without agitation until Kesho finishes and withdraws. Then Imbo and two other wolves tear at the carcass. The rest of the pack stands and waits its turn.

I've come to admire Imbo for his character. The middle-ranking male wolf, he does not seek out fights yet he stands his ground if challenged. He is handsome, moderate, and good-natured. Now he raises his head from his resting scrape, that body-sized hole wolves and dogs love to dig in the earth to curl up in. He gives me a long, quiet look. The sun and wind of bright October flow around our bodies. I have come to the fence with my recorder again, hoping to capture some howls. But it's early afternoon and there's not much activity in the pack. Still, my presence creates a stir of interest, and Naima rushes up to the fence. She cocks her head and tries to make sense of the metallic howls coming from the gray plastic box in my hands. Mephisto slinks by at a distance from the other wolves. Lailah and Kaleah run up to the fence and there is a sudden, quick quarrel as they brush against each other. But the wind blows it all clean again; the tension in the pack subsides as quickly as it rises.

You have to know the rules! Never, for instance, get down on all fours among predators. Four-leggedness might spell "prey" to wolves. On two legs, with proper knowledge, courage, and self-control, you're safe with them. It's Saturday again, and the crew of volunteers is in with the pack. Imbo has approached me in his usual friendly manner but startles me by taking my hand gently in his mouth and leading me away from the others. We don't get very far before Gale is at my side explaining this display of "parallel walking." It's a gesture of liking among wolves. Often one wolf will softly grab another's muzzle between his jaws and escort his friend away for a little tête-à-tête. I'm flattered. And I'm feeling confident. I've learned a lot about wolf behavior in my weeks at Wolf Park and I feel that the wolves accept my presence among them.

Today I've brought my camera. Soon all the wolves have followed the other volunteers to the far end of the enclosure. Only Ohtsu, the wolf who is shy of humans, remains: the perfect subject for a brief photo session. Though I know better, I kneel six feet away from him to compose the perfect photo in my lens. He's shyer than I am. If I get any closer, he'll run away. I'm just about to click the shutter when—out of nowhere—two powerful forelegs strike against my back so sharply the breath is knocked out of me. The camera falls from my hands. I'm down on all fours, and I know there's a wolf behind me waiting to see what I'll do next. But I don't know which one it is. If it's Kesho . . . a wave of fear shuts down my vocal chords. But that may be a good thing, because there's another rule: never scream when you're among wolves. High-pitched, frightened noises might provoke them to attack. And I have not been attacked, only tested. I slowly turn around to face—Imbo! He seems to be smiling at me, wagging his bushy tail. He lolls his tongue, his eyes gleam playfully. The most likable wolf in the world! Love and relief suddenly flow from my eyes in tears.

I came to the wolves in search of many things: more knowledge of them, a chance to compare my dream images with their reality, some deep truths about their nature and my own, and that of all things that still have wildness in them. In coming to Wolf Park, I left a relationship with a man who was not my parallel walker. I think I looked to the wolves to restore me to my stronger self, the one who survived a difficult childhood illness with the help of their visitations. The month has passed quickly. In these days of simple living, splendid weather, and fresh air, I have fulfilled an old, old dream. And I have gained strength.

It is my last weekend at Wolf Park. On Sunday, the park is crowded with visitors, mostly couples with young children. Pat has taken Imbo out of the enclosure on a heavy chain and stands with him in the middle of a large circle, telling anecdotes of wolf behavior in her original, observant way. I am on duty in the bookstore at the Visitors' Center. When the bookstore empties out, I lock the cashbox and head for the circle around Pat and Imbo. As I approach, Imbo suddenly strains toward me. He breaks through the circle of children and adults, pulling Pat behind him. He does not stop till he reaches me. Standing beside me, he leans his wolf shoulder against my knee and thigh. And I lay my open palm on his ample gray forehead. An energy I had not felt in many months surges into and out of my hand. Blessed connection! The universe streams about us in one unbroken flow of energy. I feel my will go out to heal the terrible rift humans have made between species. The power that arcs between hand and head, between human and wolf, is a paleolithic knowledge that we two belong together, that our two species have been together on this planet longer than any religion or philosophy of life. We must not lose this connection!

Cultivating Stony Ground
Pamela Uschuk

for Sandra Alcosser

What's resurrected marks your trail.
Hawthorne and dogwood bud near roses
you'd fenced off
with logs fat as thighs.
Beneath a pileated's staccato drill,
strawberries tendril up
through sandblonde straw.
Your seeds spite spring snow
sprouting in sun between the stones.

To your Bitterroot home I come back
from the Sonoran Desert where I learned
the fingerlight gymnastics of the coachwhip lizard,
the way rock wrens prospect adobe walls
for fire ants and dung beetles.
Scorpions flicked from the ceiling,
woke me screaming with their quick translucent tails.
But I loved the light,
a painter's inescapable light, that spoke
back from mica-jeweled soil.

II
Last winter, just one more woman
unemployed, I skidded to miss
a thick-bristled javelina who danced
into the sun in front of my car.
His tusks cut crescents
below his gray eyes

surveying each tilt of shadow he passed through.
In that waking light, he did not run
but regarded me so confidently, I'd have let him
carry me off into the mesquite.

While you fought record Louisiana floods,
I watched my chickens,
slack-beaked,
starve in the yard.
Too old and stringy to butcher,
they accused each day there were no jobs
I could stand in line for.
        Sometimes I still see their wings
like paper fans, strike
the kitchen windows as they leap
for potato peels,
the occasional empty eggshell.

III

Impermanence is our offspring.
You and I have moved so often
we haven't had the same houses
more than three years running.
Childless women, we know
impermanence is the one thing between us
that wounds and cures. We create
our lives in these rocky places.

Now, I wait for your return and walk
through violet shadows, counting
each new bloom—
thick wax crocus bells,
the stiff yellow petals of balsam root,
pasqueflowers and their submissive purple silks,
shooting stars, the blood-veined
white trumpets of Trillium above
Polygala's magenta tongues.

This far north blooms are slimmer
than the Bougainvillea's that drape, swollen
as vulva over wrought-iron rails
or the oleander's, whose slow perfume
lies dense in your Baton Rouge yard.
Palmetto bugs must swarm now,
their wings' leather flapping at your screen.
Even the moon is larger there,
a flaccid orchid slipping
between Spanish moss in bayous you canoe,
spotting egrets,
arm-thick cottonmouths
whose pink teeth open deadlier blooms.
You write that you toss
in damp sheets, dream of moldy women
while a bull alligator booms through your sleep.

Here, dusk takes the woods as a halo
charms the new moon.
Climbing the dark trail, I hear something sigh
near bear-scratchings on a Douglas fir.
My dog growls near my knee and I freeze, remembering
the black bear with the white-blazed chest
who, summer after summer, plunders your garden.
Rooting through lettuce, black raspberries or
shredding logs with his dark claws,
he always pads onto your porch
and stands erect to stare at you
through the picture window.
He seems to know when you are alone.

IV
For years I've not planted gardens,
fearing what I'd abandon,
wanting the bear to come unlured.
What I left in the desert
was there before me—
       Jimsonweed
       ocotillo

      ironwood
        yellow-flowering mesquite—
what survived overgrazing, oppressive heat.

Now, there is nothing
but the loaded ghosts of silence.
Your gardens tangle comfortably
in the woods, their roots divining water
through soil more rock than loam.
        Back from Carleton Creek,
I see plants lean to surrounding light
so each line is focused even in this dusk.
It is as if your shadow
like sudden insight passed through me
so that my movements among these plants are not my own.

This summer I will grow Nasturtiums,
maybe tomatoes and beets
against winter and its inevitable endurance.
I'll let you know how it goes.
If I should leave in the spring,
a friend, perhaps
a woman who is lost, could come
to this place where bear survive
and see what thrives, redefining
a rock-stunned barren place.

Wings

Jeane Jacobs

"Hey, Montee. Did ya pass? One more year for me and I'll be out of that joint." Pete's dark eyes flashed and he winked at me as Linda Goodhouse made her way to the back of the bus in her tight skirt.

"Sure I passed. I'll be in the tenth but I'll have English with you."

"How come?" Pete's smile changed to a slight pout. I knew it was hard on him in school. The other kids teased him about being my uncle and me being smarter in some subjects didn't help matters.

"Because my English test scores were twelfth grade level." I sat up straight, tossing my head to one side. I raised my eyebrow and watched Pete squirm.

"Smart ass," he said under his hand so Old Man Castleberry, the bus driver, wouldn't hear him cursing.

The school bus turned off the main highway just west of the river. The sunlight flickered between the trees. It wasn't moving fast enough for me, I felt like running.

"Hey, Pete. Tell Gramma I'm coming home the back way," I said as I moved to the door of the bus. I waved to the other kids and got off near the old river bridge.

"Hey, Montee, she won't like it if you're late for supper," Pete yelled out of the window as the bus sped down the blacktop road.

Carefully, I crossed the weatherworn wooden planks. Once on the other side of the bulging waters of the Arkansas River, I sat down on a boulder that stuck out over the water and took off my shoes. I stuffed my socks into black-and-white saddle oxfords, tied the strings together.

In the blue sky, between the tree branches, I noticed a hawk circling. I called to it, "Eey-hey-a-sheemanee."

I jumped down and began to run the dusty road along the river's edge. I was surrounded by wind stirring through oak leaves and the scent of cedar trees.

I ran deeper into the woods, my bare feet leaving light prints in the soft earth, the tightened muscles in my legs swiftly moving me past the caves, my breasts swaying from side to side. Salty sweat beaded my upper lip and I was breathing harder. I forced my body to make the turn up the slope before my sides would start to ache.

At the top of the hill, I could see the small clearing we called the sacred place. Slowing to catch my breath, I looked up to see the hawk just above me. It called to me, "Heok, he-ook."

I lowered myself down into the soft spring grass in the center of the clearing. I lay on my back, staring into the flickering light through the trees. Streaks of sweat poured down my back from my armpits. The new grass was cool against me. The earth seemed to mold around my body. The hawk's voice echoed in my ears. The soft sound of her wings pulled at my soul. The smell of cedar trees reminded me of the first time Great-grandmother Haloka brought me into the woods.

I was around eight and a little frightened of her. The other kids told me to watch out for the tricky old woman. They said she was crazy. But my Choctaw Gramma told me to always respect my elders, even the Cherokee ones.

Haloka's face had creasing lines around deep gray eyes and a wide white smile. She took my hand and said, "It's time you know some things, Montee."

We walked the path into the wooded area behind our place. I felt a heated tingle between our hands as we went along the river where the soft clay oozed between my toes.

Sparrows chirped to the beat of a solitary woodpecker. Sunlight flickered through the wide branches of the tall cedars. Finally we came to a clearing within a small circle of trees. The smell of cedar filled the air, and sunlight shone directly over our heads.

Haloka stood tall, her leather-moccasined feet firmly on the ground. I could see the shadows of her parted legs through her long full skirt.

"We have come to this sacred place so I can show you the ways," she said, raising her arms toward the heavens. She bent her knees slightly and began to shout, "Thank you, O Great-grandfather, for you have given me this day. Thank you, Mighty Ancestors, for your blood flowing through my veins. Thank you, Earth Mother, for your strength. I have come to this place to share the ways with our Great-granddaughter. Thank you for your guidance. My heart is full."

She began singing words in her Cherokee language, moving her arms from side to side, as she bounced to the beat of a silent drum. My own heart kept time to her musical chant.

Shafts of shimmering light loomed between the trees falling around Haloka's shoulders. She shook the owl-faced rattle with small jerks and yelled after each verse, "Eeh Ya. Eeh Ya HO."

Wiping her forehead with a small red cloth, she sat on a freshly cut tree stump. "Bring me some rocks, my child." She held her tanned hands wide open facing each other to demonstrate the size she wanted. "Be sure they are alive."

I figured she meant the warm rocks were the live ones. I searched for the stones that had been in the sun, carrying them to her in twos. She placed them in a space she prepared for each one by sweeping the ground smooth. These stones formed a large circle.

"Now bring me four big ones." She seemed pleased with my ability to choose live rocks.

The four rocks were placed outside the circle. One at the top of the circle was north. One at the bottom was south. The others were east and west. She told me to sit inside the circle to the south facing inward. She sat to the north facing me.

Haloka sat quietly with her eyes closed for a moment, breathing in deep breaths of air and blowing them out. She laid a square piece of leather on the ground in front of her. On the leather she placed her rattle, a small clay bowl, a feather fan, and a soft leather beaded pouch.

"We are of the Bird Clan. My mother's people was of the Bird Clan and my father's mother's people was of the Bird Clan." She took a clump of dry leaves from her leather pouch and crumbled them into the round bowl as she continued unfolding her story to me.

"The women have passed down spirits of flight. There must be wisdom used with this freedom. Montee, these ways are sacred.

You was chosen as a baby to be taught the beliefs of our clan."

Haloka took a small box of matches from her skirt pocket, lighting the leaves in the clay bowl. They smoldered and began to smoke. She made circular motions in front of her, as if to pull the smoke into her body. Then she set the bowl in front of me.

"Here, child, you must cleanse yourself with this sacred smoke. I will help you see your spirit truth."

I made the motions the same way Haloka had done, hoping the other kids weren't right about her being crazy, half wishing that what she said was true, that I was a chosen one.

The fresh cedar scent and the dry smoke filled my nostrils as I pulled the smoke into me with my hands. Haloka smiled and chanted a song softly to herself. I listened closely as she told me of her belief.

"Myself, I have the spirit of a great white owl." As I looked into her gray eyes, I could see the glistening white owl's wings spread in flight.

"The owl glides for great distances without moving its wings. It can climb high above the earth." Haloka made movements with her arms demonstrating the wing motions.

She sat there, her back straight, her face sparkling with pride. "The owl lives a long life with freedom of flight, which gives my heart great joy."

She crumbled a few more leaves into the bowl, lifting it to her and blowing into the tiny sparks until they smoked. She began to wave the feather fan over the smoke and circled it over my head.

"Close your eyes, Montee. Concentrate on the white light inside your head. This is your spirit eye."

The feather fan brushed my face as I squeezed my eyes shut. Without hearing a sound I felt her hand touch mine. A warm powerful touch. I knew I was safe in the midst of her magic.

"Think of nothing, Montee. Do you see the white spot?" she asked me quietly.

I forced the word to come out, "Yes."

There was the whitest light inside my head, a swishing sound like running water in my ears. Suddenly, I was free with the soft sound of moving wings in the wind.

"Eeh—you are a spotted hawk, Montee," softly she whispered.

I swooped high above the earth into the bluest sky. The ground below me appeared to be a great patchwork quilt, like the ones Aunt Lela made. Trees swayed in the breeze. Rolling hills blended together in colors of brown and green. The great waters of the Arkansas River flowed swiftly like rushing foam. I glided freely through white puffy clouds. The wind caressed my face. I knew I was a brown spotted hawk. I had always known.

Below me, two coyotes rested in the sun. With my hawk eyes, I watched field mice racing through the grass to hide themselves. I swooped closer to the earth over the roof of our house. Gramma was working in the garden. I made noises with my hawk voice to get her to notice. She didn't look up.

A gust of wind caused my wing feathers to flutter as I saw the circle of trees. A soft voice said, "It is time to return."

A tingling sensation started at the top of my head and a slight rumble filled my ears. I was back in the circle. The old Cherokee woman laughed and laughed.

It was Pete's laughter I heard as I opened my eyes and squinted toward the setting sun.

"What's ya doin' on the ground in the middle of this spooky place? Ain't this the circle that Ol' Cherokee Haloka comes to when she works her spells?" Pete said, his eyes looking around as if he might see something magical. "Ma says for ya to quit foolin' 'round and get home."

I jumped to my feet and grabbed my shoes. "I'll race ya to the back door. I'll even give you a head start," I said looking into Pete's dark eyes. "Ten paces."

His wide brown feet hit the path. "You're on." His black ponytail swayed back and forth across his back. I studied his stride, knobby knees bowing inward as the calves of his legs shot out behind him.

Excitement raced through me. I actually gave him fifteen paces before I took off. I pulled my arms in tight against my ribs with my fists clenched as I caught up to Pete. I ran along beside him for awhile to make him feel he might have a chance. He tried to keep pace. Gramma said Pete takes after her, he just doesn't have the heart of a runner.

We reached the front of the barn. My heart was pounding, a voice in my head said, "Okay, Hawk, break away." I bolted out ahead of him with smooth swift strides, lifting my knees higher and kicking my feet out in front of me. The strength of my hawk spirit drove the heaviness out of my burning thighs.

I turned to see how far ahead I was; through the dust-filled air, Pete looked as if he were standing still. I tagged the back step almost a hundred yards ahead of him.

I looked up into the sky at the brown spotted hawk diving and circling as she called out her victory cry.

Pete's face was red with sweat dripping from his black hair. "Shit, girl. I ain't never beat ya. Well, ya didn't beat me as bad as the last time." He smiled the soft smile like Gramma's as if it didn't really matter. "Guess the Ol' Cherokee was right, Montee. Ya got wings on your feet."

A Story of a Girl and Her Dog

Alix Kates Shulman

Lucky Larrabee was an only child, and unpredictable. At eight, she was still trying to sail down from the garage roof with an umbrella. She never ate ice cream without a pickle. She was afraid of nothing in the world except three boys in her class and her uncle Len who patted her funny. She brought home every stray dog in the neighborhood. She upset the assistant principal by participating in the Jewish Affair.

Naturally her parents worried; but they adored her nevertheless and all the more.

There is little Lucky, wearing red anklets with stripes down the sides and poorly tied brown oxfords while everyone else has on loafers, her hair hanging down in strings, her chin thrust out, absolutely refusing to sing the words, Jesus or Christ. Why? Two Jewish girls in her class will not sing, and though she has never been Jewish before, Lucky has joined them. She says it is a free country and you can be anything you like. I'm a Jew, she says and will not sing Jesus.

Everyone knows she's no more Jewish than their teacher. It is ridiculous! But she insists and what can they do? She is ruining the Christmas Pageant. They'll get her at recess, they'll get her after school, they'll plant bad pictures in her desk, they'll think of something. But it won't work. Incorrigible little fanatic!

Okay. She doesn't have to sing. But will she just mouth the words silently during the program please? No one will have to know.

No, she won't. If they try to make her, she swears she'll hold her breath until she faints instead. Perhaps she'll do it anyway!

Perhaps she'll hold it till she's dead! That'll show them who's a Jew and who isn't.

Is something wrong at home, Mrs. Larrabee? Does Lucky eat a good enough breakfast? Get enough sleep? She is very thin. Has she grown thinner? Not meaning to alarm you, but Lucky has been unusually sullen in class lately—doesn't participate in the class discussions as she used to, doesn't volunteer her answers, no longer seems interested in current events, spends too much time daydreaming, picking at scabs, being negative. She doesn't seem to be trying. Her fingernails. Is there any known source of tension at home? The school likes to be kept informed about these matters as we try to keep parents informed about progress at school. Don't you agree, parents and teachers ought to be working closely together in harmony, for the benefit of the child. The only concrete suggestion the school can make at this time is some companionship and diversion for Lucky. Another child perhaps, or a dog. Meanwhile, we'll just keep an eye on her. Thank you so much for coming in. These conferences are always helpful in any case, even if they do no more than clear the air.

As the Larrabees had been half considering buying a dog for Christmas anyway, they decided it would do no harm to seem accommodating and took the step. They waited until a month had elapsed after the Christmas Pageant so Lucky would not suspect a connection, and then, piling into the new family Nash, backing out of the cinder drive, they drove straight out on Main Street beyond the city limits and continued on into the country to buy a dog.

Naturally, Lucky was permitted by the concerned Larrabees to pick out the pup herself, with only one restriction. It had to be a boy dog, they said, because if they took home a girl dog, sooner or later they would have to have her spayed, which would be cruel and unnatural and would make her into a fat, lazy, and unhappy bitch, or they'd have to let her have babies. For keeping her locked up during heat (also cruel and unnatural) couldn't be expected to work forever; creatures have a way of eluding their jailors in quest of forbidden knowledge—witness the fate of Sleeping Beauty, Bluebeard's wives, etc., and the unwanted litters of the neighborhood bitches. And if they let her go ahead and have her babies, well, either they'd have to keep the puppies (a certain portion of which could be expected to be female too), generating an unmanageable amount of work, anxiety, and expense, even supposing they had the facilities, which of course they did not. Or they'd have to wrench the pups away from their mother (equally cruel and unnatural as well as a bad example for a child) and worry about finding a decent home for each of them besides. No, no, it could be any pup she chose as long as it was male.

The seven mongrel puppies from which she was permitted to choose one were to her untutored eyes and arms indistinguishable as to sex unless she deliberately looked. So she was perfectly happy to restrict her choice to the four males, though she did feel sorry for the females who, it seemed, were condemned to suffer a cruel and unnatural life or else bring on, like Eve, more trouble than they were worth—particularly since cuddling them in the hollow between her neck and shoulder felt quite as wonderful as cuddling the males. But such, she accepted, was family life.

She chose neither the runt she was temperamentally drawn to but upon whom her father frowned, nor the jumper of the litter over whom her mother voiced certain reasonable reservations, but instead picked from the two remaining males the long-eared, thoughtful-eyed charmer who endeared himself to her by stepping across three of his siblings as though they were stepping stones in order to reach her eager fingers wiggling in the corner of the box and investigate them with his adorable wet nose. Curiosity: the quality her parents most admired in Lucky herself. He sniffed and then licked her fingers in a sensual gesture she took for friendship, and although she continued to examine all the pups for a considerable time, picking them up and cuddling them individually, deliberating at length before rendering her final decision, she knew very early the one she would take home. It pained her to reject the others, particularly the runt and a certain female who tickled her neck lovingly when she held her up and was pure when she peeked underneath. But by eight Lucky had already learned through experience that one could not have everything one wanted, that every choice entailed the rejection of its alternatives, and that if she didn't hurry up and announce her selection, much as she enjoyed playing with all the puppies, she'd provoke her father's pique and lose the opportunity to decide herself.

She named the dog Skippy because of the funny way he bounced when he walked. An unimaginative name perhaps, but direct (a quality she instinctively valued) and to her inexperienced mind which did not know that the dog would stop bouncing once it got a few months older, appropriate. Her parents thought she might have selected a name with more flair, but naturally they said nothing.

The day of Lucky's brightening (her word, for no one ever taught her another) seemed like an ordinary late-summer Saturday. Unsuspectingly, she was just finishing a treasured bath, where she had spent a long time sending the water back and forth between the sides of the tub to simulate ocean waves. She was studying the movement of the water, its turbulence, its cresting at the edges and doubling back, trying to imagine how the process could possibly illuminate, as her father declared, the mysteries of the ocean's waves and tides; and afterward when her brain had grown weary of encompassing the continental coasts, which she had never seen, the earth and the moon, she filled her washcloth with puffs of air which she could pop out in little explosions into the water sending big bubbles rippling through the bath like porpoises.

Up through the open bathroom window drifted the familiar sounds of her father setting up the barbecue in the backyard and her mother bringing out the fixings on a tray. Next door Bertie Jones was still mowing the lawn while from the Jones' screened-in porch the ballgame droned on. Summer days; dog days.

Lucky climbed reluctantly from the tub, now cold, and examined herself in the mirror. Whistle gap between her front teeth, a splash of freckles, short protruding ears, alert: Lucky herself. If she had known what delights awaited her in the next room, she would not have lingered to peel a strip of burnt skin from her shoulder or scratch open a mosquito bite. But she was a nervous child who had never, from the day she learned to drop things over the edge of her high chair for her mother to retrieve, been able to let well enough alone. Three full minutes elapsed before she finally wrapped herself in a towel and padded into her bedroom where Skip, banished from the backyard during dinner preparations, awaited her with wagging tail.

"Skippy Dip!" she cried, dropping to her knees, and throwing her arms around him. She hugged his neck and he licked her face in a display of mutual affection.

She tossed the towel at the door, sat down on the maple vanity bench, made a moue at her freckly face in the mirror, and in a most characteristic pursuit, lifted her left foot to the bench to examine an interesting blister on her big toe, soaked clean and plump in her long bath.

Suddenly Skip's wet little nose, as curious as on the day they had met, delved between her legs with several exploratory sniffs.

"Skip!" Lucky giggled in mock dismay. "Get out of there," pushing his nose aside and quickly lowering her foot, for she did know a little. Skip retreated playfully but only until Lucky returned (inevitably) to the blister. For like any pup who has not yet completed his training, he could hardly anticipate every consequence or generalize from a single instance. You know how a dog longs to sniff at things. When Lucky's knee popped up again, exposing that interesting smell, Skip's nose returned as though invited.

Suddenly Lucky felt a new intriguing sensation. *"What's this?"*

She had once, several years earlier, felt another strange sensation in the groin, one that had been anything but pleasant. She and Judy Jones, the girl next door, had been playing mother and baby in a game of House. As Lucky lay on the floor of that very room having her "diaper" changed by a maternal Judy, the missing detail to lend a desired touch of verisimilitude to the game struck Lucky. "Baby powder!" she cried. "Sprinkle on some baby powder!"

"Baby powder?" blinked Judy.

"Get the tooth powder from the bathroom shelf. The Dr. Lyons."

In the first contact with Skip's wet nose, Lucky remembered her words as if they still hung in the room. She didn't stop to remember the intervening events: how Judy obediently went to the bathroom but couldn't find the Dr. Lyons; how, after finally finding it she could barely manage to get the tin open. Lucky's memory flashed ahead to the horrible instant when the astringent powder fell through the air from a great (but not sufficiently great) height onto the delicate tissue of her inner labia and stung her piercingly, provoking a scream that brought her poor mother running anxiously from a distant room.

But the sensation produced by her pal Skippy was in every respect different. It was cool not hot; insinuating not shocking; cozy, provocative, delicious. It drew her open and out, not closed in retreat. No scream ensued; only the arresting thought, *What's this?* Like the dawning of a new idea or the grip of that engaging question, What makes it tick? If she had had the movable ears of her friend's species, they would have perked right up. *What's this?* The fascination of beginnings, the joy of the new. Something more intriguing than a blister.

She touched Skip's familiar silky head tentatively, but this time did not quite push it away. And he, enjoying the newness too (he was hardly more than a pup), sniffed and then, bless him, sniffed again. And following the natural progression for a normally intelligent dog whose interest has been engaged—as natural and logical as the human investigator's progress from observed phenomenon to initial hypothesis to empirical test—the doggie's pink tongue followed his nose's probe with a quizzical exploratory lick.

What would her poor parents have thought if they had peeked in? They would have known better than to see or speak evil, for clearly these two young creatures, these trusting pups (of approximately the same ages when you adjust for species), were happy innocents. They would probably have blamed themselves for having insisted on a male pup. They might even have taken the poor animal to the gas chambers of the ASPCA and themselves to some wildly expensive expert who would only confuse and torment them with impossibly equivocal advice until they made some terrible compromise. At the very least, there would have been furious efforts at distraction and that night much wringing of hands.

Fortunately our Adam and Eve remain alone to pursue their pragmatic investigations. The whole world is before them.

The charcoal is now ready to take on the weenies. Mrs. Larrabee kisses her husband affectionately on the neck as she crosses the yard toward the house. She opens the screen door, leans inside, and yells up the stairs, "Dinner."

"Just a minute," says Lucky, squeezing her eyes closed. One more stroke of that inquisitive tongue—only one more!—and Lucky too will possess as her own one of nature's most treasured recipes.

Waves and oceans, suns and moons, barbecues, bubbles, blisters, tongues and tides—what a rich banquet awaits the uncorrupted.

Is Holly Working Today?
Barbara J. Wood

For Holly and me it started with a stray kitten. Of course, the benefits to people of having animal companions were known at least as long ago as the earliest written histories. In ancient Egypt dog-headed Anubis was the physician and apothecary to the gods. The dog was the sacred emblem of the Sumerian goddess-physician Gula. Dogs were kept at the shrine of Asklepios in Greece, and the healing power of their licking wounds was renowned. The Gaulish Goddess Sequane recommended holding puppies to one's body to absorb the ills.

In the eighteenth century, it was reported from the York Retreat in England that patients benefited from caring for rabbits and poultry. By 1867, in Bethel, Germany, epileptics were seen to improve with horseback riding and the association of companion animals. Germans developed guide dogs for blind veterans after World War I. Horses, dogs, and farm animals served in rehabilitation programs at the U.S. Army Air Force Convalescent Center in Pawling, New York, after World War II. In 1966 Erling Stordahl, the blind director of the rehabilitation center in Bertostoln, Norway, began employing dogs and horses with the blind and physically handicapped. In 1969 Dr. Boris Levinson, the first child psychologist in the United States to use and promote pet-facilitated therapy, wrote of his experiences with his cotherapist Jingles in his book *Pet-Oriented Child Psychotherapy*. But the possibilities for my own professional work were not brought home to me until an abandoned kitten was found huddled in the winter weather on the front steps of the elementary school for emotionally disturbed children where I provide therapy three days a week.

The principal brought the homeless kitten to my office until other arrangements could be made. The children who came to my office while the kitten was there immediately brightened and chatted easily. Moved by the children's positive transformation, I wrote a proposal to the school authorities and received permission for my dog Holly to accompany me during counseling sessions.

I knew that Holly, a seven-year-old spayed female of mixed parentage who tips the scales at nineteen pounds, would be perfect for the job. After all, this was the dog who allowed the new kitten to chew on her ears. She is tolerant, gregarious, excellent on a leash, and in general, I thought, well behaved. Although she was not reared with children, Holly has had ample exposure to them, so sticky fingers in her short brown fur would not come as a shock. She loves to ride in the car, an essential trait if she was to accompany me to the school on a regular basis. She had additional qualifications in knowing the standard commands "sit," "shake," "lie down," "come," and "speak" in English and in Spanish.

Preparations were made at school. The children made signs for my office doors: "Holly is happy to be here." I installed a dog bed and bowls for dry dog chow and water. Holly has always enjoyed an open bowl policy at home, and the same seemed appropriate for her at work. I also secured a supply of doggy treats (the cereal-based multicolored ones) in case all went wrong and I was reduced to bribery. Holly and I were both going to be on trial.

My supervisor had made her lack of enthusiasm for the "experiment" quite clear with her curt questions: "What if 'it' bit one of the children?" "What if 'it' had an 'accident'?" I had submitted a ten-page proposal, which included a veterinarian's certification that Holly was free of disease or parasites and a testament to her even temperament, and all I could think of during this inquisition (but did not say) was, "What if one of those emotionally disturbed children bites Holly?" "Can Holly get a disease from a child?" Fortunately the other administrators, especially the principal, were supportive, and Holly and I were scheduled to begin.

I don't know if Holly knew we were embarking on a new life, but I did. I had thought I had enough worries even before my supervisor made it abundantly clear that any problems whatsoever resulting from the "dog experiment" would reflect on me. I bought Holly a new leash and collar, gave her a bath, shined her name, rabies, and license tags, and we were off.

Holly was excited. She had never before been invited to get in the car when I was going to work. With purse, briefcase, lunch, and case notes, I didn't seem to have a hand free for her leash, but despite her harried mistress, Holly made a bright entrance at school. All went well until we reached the tile floor in the hall.

Holly has never liked linoleum, preferring carpeting like that at home, which gives her better footing. While she slipped and slid her way beside me down the hall, quivering but dutiful, it dawned on me that for all the preparations I had made, I had overlooked the most important one—of Holly herself. I had reviewed the literature on pet-facilitated therapy. I had cleared the idea with the teaching staff and the teachers' union and assured the janitor that Holly was house trained and would cause him no extra work. I had discussed Holly's arrival with my little counselees and checked for allergies. Citing our rodent predecessors (many classrooms already harbored hamsters, guinea pigs, and gerbils), I had gained administrative support and official approval. The only one I had not consulted was Holly.

Half an hour remained before the children arrived. An announcement over the public address system alerted us there would be a fire drill that day. I gave Holly a treat; I could have used one myself, thinking of all the things there are in an institutional school setting for a house dog to adjust to: long stretches of tile floors, bells, the public address system, one hundred and twenty children changing classes, school buses roaring up, children yelling and shouting in the gym just down the hall, and the smells of disinfectant and strangers. And now the fire drill. I knew I should have brought Holly for a site visit over the weekend to familiarize her with the building at least, the largest she had ever seen.

My first counselee of the day knocked on the door. Holly barked as she does at home for the mail carrier, which is to say loudly and with conviction. I would have to talk to Holly about that—greeting insecure children with aggressive barking was, to say the least, therapeutically counterproductive.

I opened the door. A small boy entered, and he and Holly stared at each other warily. He asked, "Does that dog bite?" I suggested he might like to give Holly a treat. He could pick any color he liked. He chose red. Holly has always been very careful and gentle in taking food from someone's hand. She has a soft mouth. As the boy stretched out his hand rather uncertainly, Holly neatly and gently took the treat, swallowed it, and licked his other hand. The crucial moment passed: they were friends. The meaning of the term "companion animal" became clear to me. "Companion" comes from the Latin, *com*, meaning "with," and *panis*, meaning "bread." A companion is someone you share food with. I saw this bond, so important throughout human history, at work before my eyes: the boy realizing Holly's teeth were no threat, that she would not bite, that she appreciated the treat, licking his other hand and looking for more. Her tongue and wagging tail said to the boy she accepted him. For some of the children at the school, Holly's would be the first unconditional acceptance they had ever experienced.

After a succession of little visitors came to our door at the sound of the bell, Holly realized that bells and boys (there are very few girls in this school) meant treats. She had found a gravy train. She soaked up the attention. She had never been petted or treated so much in her life. Then came the fire drill.

The fire department requires monthly drills. The staff is alerted that a drill may be held sometime during the day, but not when. Sometimes the fire department calls a surprise drill. At least I knew this one was coming.

The fire bell is intended to be loud, both piercing and alarming. Its maker would be pleased to know that this school's bell probably exceeds the requirements. I thought the sound would be bad enough, but Holly would also have to traverse the slippery tile floors, smelling so strongly of disinfectant, and go down a flight of metal stairs booming and echoing with the footsteps of hurrying children and staff. All timed by a stop watch. No one likes fire drills, especially in winter, and it was now winter. An unsuccessful fire drill had to be reported and repeated under fire department supervision. It leaves a mark on the record. If there were any problems, Holly could be branded a fire hazard.

The alarm went off. Holly's ears went straight up, an appreciable feat for a floppy-eared dog. I grabbed her leash, snapped it on the stunned dog, put my other arm around the counselee and told both in my most authoritative voice to *Come*. I turned off the lights behind us and closed the door, as the fire code requires. We started down a hall wet from the snow tramped in from afternoon recess. Holly needed more than four feet to stay upright on her own, but the crowd pushed her close to me. The stairs thundered. Holly went rigid. "COME NOW!" That or be trampled. Holly, who is a smallish dog, took the stairs in three leaps, dragging the boy and me behind her. We made it outside and in line just under the wire. We would not have to repeat the drill. There would be no black mark against the school. Holly has never grown happy with fire drills, but the wild eyes, heaving sides, and terror have subsided with time. That first day was quite literally a trial by fire, but we passed.

On the following days, Holly willingly got in the car to go to work. She improved her greeting behavior until she became irresistible. She learned not to bark at a knock on the office door. I trimmed her nails short so her pads get more traction on the tile floors. I found a large piece of carpeting for my office so she can be more comfortable there, and now the children can sit on the floor to pet, brush, play with, talk to, and confide in her. She licks them all; adults my be inclined to wash off dog saliva, but to the kids it's liquid gold.

Holly has developed her own fan club. The counselees adore her, and the other children cluster at our office door in the morning to pet her and say hi. The same happens in reverse in the afternoon before the kids go home. Holly also makes class visits and has helped many a class reach a behavioral goal. Teachers come in for "pet therapy" as well. A short pat is restorative after a long day.

When a new student comes to the school, a "veteran" student gives the child a guided tour. Holly is the first stop. Parents report how the "shrink dog" is talked about at home. When one class began a pen pal project with an out-of-state school, Holly was the subject of their letters. Before Holly started at the school, some students tried to bribe me by offering fifty cents to get them for counseling during the time for their English or math test. Now Holly is offered a dollar.

I have become invisible at the other end of the leash. I didn't know how much so until I caught strep throat from one of my "huggers" (an occupational hazard when working with children) and missed two days of work. When I called in sick the first day, I was asked if that meant Holly would be staying home too. The second day I was asked if I could at least send Holly to work in a cab. It was not an unserious suggestion. The staff did not want to spend another day answering the question, "Is Holly working today?"

Holly does work! Three months into the project, nine-year-old LeMar, a third grader who had been one of Holly's regulars, was shot and killed. A "boyfriend" apparently went "mad" and shot LeMar's mother four times. When, hearing his mother's screams, LeMar came out of his bedroom, he was shot dead. From their school bus, the other children saw the police and ambulance and the coroner taking LeMar's body away. By the time the children arrived at school, they were thoroughly frightened and in tears.

Holly and I went down to LeMar's classroom. LeMar's teacher, a woman in her early twenties, said with tears streaming down her face that her educational degree had not prepared her to handle a situation like this. One of the local television station's remote satellite vans was circling the building, no doubt hoping for pictures of sobbing children to increase their ratings. The children were crying for LeMar and because their teacher was crying and because they feared the same fate for themselves. Their lives were just as precarious as LeMar's in a world where men and guns rule.

Nothing prepares you for a situation like this. But we were in it. First we talked about how crying was perfectly okay for adults and children alike, especially over something like the senseless killing of a nine-year-old boy in his pajamas. Being scared was okay too. Gunshots in the dark are something to be scared of. Intense feelings are normal—being able to feel is the essence of being human. The children calmed as we talked about missing LeMar. We wrote letters to LeMar's mother in the hospital (she survived the shooting), telling our sorrow about LeMar's death. It was when the crying had subsided somewhat that I realized what Holly had been doing.

Holly had worked her way around the room, going from child to child (and to the teacher), putting her front paws on their laps, stretching up and licking the tears from their faces. Many embraced her, running their fingers through her fur with an intensity that would have left her bald if it had continued all day. With her touch and tongue, Holly consoled each child on a deeper level than could ever be possible with words coming from an adult associated with the terrifying world. Through that dark day, and later at the funeral, and through the lingering sadness, Holly provided more comfort than anyone or anything else. It was draining work for her. She fell asleep on the back seat of the car before we even left the parking lot that day.

Holly does hard physical work as well. When the good weather began, each counselee wanted to take Holly for a walk. We would walk around the block and romp on the grassy area of the playground. The brief respite from the structure of school made for relaxed counseling. Holly soon trained each child how to go for a sniff around the neighborhood. Holly became quite a child trainer. In her own self-defense, lest the children run her ragged doing tricks hour after hour, she convinced them that she did not know how to "sit," "speak," "lie down," or "shake hands"; she now taught them to follow her on the leash as she checked out an interesting smell here or a fascinating odor there. When playing chase, she knew just how fast to go to stay out of reach, while staying close enough to keep the game interesting. She knows the border of the playground, so no one gets too close to the street. On really active days, Holly also falls asleep on the back seat of the car on the way home. Some days I could join her. Maybe we could both use a cab.

Holly's fame spread. The school newsletter featured her in a full-page article. The newsletter editor alerted neighborhood newspapers, the city newspaper, and television news departments. But fame and success do not always bring appreciation. My supervisor "discovered" that end-of-the-year paperwork would take an extra day a week in the office to complete. One of Holly's days was cut. It seemed that if the "canine counselor" got any more publicity, we might face further cuts. Holly already whimpered on the two days she had to stay home when I went to work. I was disappointed, Holly pined, and the kids were depressed.

Evaluation of the counselees indicated that the "dog experiment" had made a positive difference. There were 10.3 percent fewer absences, and disruptive behaviors were less extreme. These are children who could not function in a regular class setting, the "throwaways" of our disposable society. These children, on their own, got together a petition about Holly. It was badly typed, miserably spelled—and wonderful. Children who could hardly get along on a one-to-one basis and were disastrous in a group cooperated in this effort, assigned their best (and only) typist, worked out the wording of their demands, and collected signatures. I only got wind of it when they asked me for the name of the program supervisor. I gave it to them.

Their petition was ignored, which was worse even than its being rejected. But I was not fired, and Holly was not branded a health or fire hazard. The kids learned that spelling, writing, and the other hated English lessons could have a meaning outside of the classroom and, even more important, that they could work together without hitting and kicking. Of course, it would have been better if the petition had been taken seriously, but Holly and I are still there, and lobbying continues for the project's permanence and expansion.

I work with human emotions. I am trained in helping people reach and maintain emotional well-being. I am paid for this work. Holly does the same work: like most companion animals, she attends to the emotional well-being of people. She is not paid though the work she is doing in a professional setting at school is well beyond her responsibilities as a private house dog. I do not know how to recompense her for this additional labor, and probably most people would consider even the idea of compensation ridiculous. I was already giving her a kind and loving home with good food and regular medical care, and I have not been able to think of any improvements or extras that she might enjoy.

I am concerned about the ethics of my turning Holly into a "professional" dog. I am scrupulously careful that Holly is not abused by the children although that has been easy so far, since no child has to date ever attempted to harm her. Only on one occasion have I asked her to go to school when she may not have wanted to. Freezing rain was coming down, monsoon-fashion, when she went out in the morning to do her business. She came back in and went back to bed. It was an intelligent assessment of the day. If I had had the choice, I would have gone back to bed too. But when I called Holly to get into the car, she came, so off to work we went. I felt guilty, however. When I am ill, I call in sick. Can Holly call in sick? Does she have an obligation as a professional to continue, regardless of her feelings and needs, with what she has taken on?

Holly responds eagerly when I ask, "Do you want to go to school today?" She has become more assured and self-assertive than she was before. She takes less guff off the cats at home and now deals easily with the slippery floors and metal stairs at school. She handles the children with confidence and sensitivity. Her unconditional acceptance of the kids reduces their tension and anxiety and consequently makes counseling less stressful for all concerned. She makes my job easier and more enjoyable. She looks like she is enjoying herself.

So the answer to the question "Is Holly working today?" is "Yes, as long as she seems to want to." May the Dog Deities of ancient times smile upon her and her work.

No Greater Gift
Margo Gathright-Dietrich

"And Margo, you get Wallaby."
My least favorite of the dogs. My tenth choice of the ten. The laziest. The least attentive and responsive. The worst.

"Be professional," the trainers ordered. My thoughts raced. Professional what? I'm a professional nurse. Perhaps even a "professional" disabled person. And though I have experience obedience training dogs and their owners, I didn't feel like a professional dog trainer or even a professional dog handler. And I wanted Ontario, a beautiful, responsive male golden retriever. If they saw that in my face I might not get *any* dog.

"Show your dog how much you love it," the trainers demanded. "Remember, these dogs can read you like a book. That leash is like a wick—everything you're thinking and feeling goes right down it to your dog. Sixty-five to eighty percent of what you get from your dog has come from you." I took Wallaby's leash and slipped the loop over my left wrist brace, snugly closing the velcro. Trying to smile and hide my disappointment, I looked at *my* dog. She slouched on her left hip and turned her head away from me. All around us the other dogs were standing, wagging their tails, kissing their people. The people were grinning, ohing and ahing, kissing their dogs. I wanted to cry.

Wallaby wouldn't even acknowledge me. Again, my mind raced—that indecisive, unorganized thinking one does when feeling insecure. Wallaby hadn't responded well to any of the participants—she watched her trainers. Should I feed her? No, they'd said, "No treats." How did the trainers pet her? Maybe she doesn't like my touch. Maybe it's my wheelchair. But she hadn't worked for the "walkies" either. She looks as miserable as I feel! What, I brooded, would make her happy?

It had been nine months since I applied for a service dog.

After seeing a promo for a television news story on dogs trained to help the physically impaired, I had put a tape in the VCR and eagerly awaited that evening's *20/20*. "Wonder Dogs" overwhelmed me.

Canine Companions for Independence, a private, nonprofit organization, was founded in 1975 by Bonita Bergin, who, while touring Asia, observed disabled people getting about with the help of burros. She believed that many similar people, frequently placed in institutions in the United States, could manage their own lives if they had suitable assistance. She set out to prove that dogs, with their unique working qualities, could learn to be arms and legs for people using wheelchairs. The first Canine Companion was placed with a quadriplegic woman in 1976; that was about five hundred dogs ago.

CCI breeds puppies from pedigreed dogs carefully chosen to be loving, intelligent, responsible, sensitive animals in peak physical condition. When the puppies are eight weeks old, they're placed in foster homes where they're socialized and taught forty obedience commands. At about eighteen months of age, they return to a CCI kennel (two in California, one in Ohio, one in New York, with more planned in other states) for advanced training in the forty-nine specialized commands they'll use to assist their disabled partners. These include turning light switches on and off, pushing elevator buttons, pulling manual wheelchairs, and retrieving all manner of dropped items. They also assist with shopping and banking errands by standing up on their hind legs and using their mouths to give the clerks money and receive small packages or deposit slips. And the dogs learn how to learn—so they will learn new tasks as needs arise. The television program emphasized that a dog's blue and yellow backpack, "which carries everything from school books and medication to a few dog biscuits," is a badge of "exceptional merit" awarded only to those who graduate to a partnership with a physically impaired person. The backpack serves to tell the dog it's on duty and to let people know this is a "working dog."

These dogs cannot be purchased. They must be *earned* by the disabled person who, with the dog, completes CCI's two week training course, dubbed Boot Camp. It's a grueling schedule of lectures (on canine psychology, resistance and correction; veterinary health care; home and public safety; and learning theory) with long practice hours for the humans to learn how to get the dogs to perform the eighty-nine tasks the dogs have previously learned. And to perform them in all types of places and situations.

I immediately fell in love with the concept. Years ago, during obedience training classes, I had worked with many dogs. But these companion animals had talents and abilities beyond anything I had ever witnessed. I wanted one to help me find new ways of doing things.

Six years ago, I experienced my first symptoms of Post-Polio Syndrome, a slowly progressive disease that, for some who had polio, appears about thirty years after the initial virus. I went from a "normal" life of wife, homemaker, full-time career psychiatric nurse, weekend hiker, swimmer, tennis player, do-anything-I-wanted-to-do-person, to (by the time I trained with Wallaby) an electric three-wheel scooter user, too weak to work, often-needing-help-with-everyday-household-tasks-(gulp)-disabled-person. My symptoms include muscle weakness, muscle and joint pain, intolerance to cold, and debilitating fatigue that comes on without warning—the way a marathon runner feels on "hitting the wall," only in my case it can result from activities no more strenuous than getting dressed or walking through my home. Four months after I first saw "Wonder Dogs," I began to need help in public rest rooms that lacked raised toilets. This was one place my husband couldn't help. It was embarrassing to ask strangers to pull me off the pot. And sometimes (out of their own fear or embarrassment) they would say "No" or ignore me.

I completed CCI's lengthy application procedure and was put on a waiting list for Boot Camp. Often depressed by what was happening to my body and, as a result, my life, I dreamed of the day my dog would give me back some of my independence. To lift my spirits, I used creative visualization to picture a dog helping me, for example, pulling me to a standing from a sitting position. I showed the "Wonder Dogs" video to anyone who would watch, and sometimes I watched it alone, tears streaming down my face, as I looked forward to when *my* dog would help restore my dignity.

In April 1989, I learned that the Virginia Federation of Women's Clubs had donated money to sponsor a CCI dog for a Virginian. I called the Federation's president. She called CCI, and three weeks later I drove my specially equipped van to Ohio for Boot Camp.

On my nervous arrival at the training center, I immediately received a stern lecture about being fifteen minutes late—that was not responsible behavior and only responsible people got dogs. The trainer didn't want to hear my explanation. I apologized and promised it would not happen again. "Good," she said briefly. I began to understand the term Boot Camp.

I stole a quick look around the room and saw a man in a manual wheelchair, a woman on a three-wheel electric scooter similar to mine, two ambulatory women, a ten-year-old girl and a seven-year-old-boy—these two in electric wheelchairs. The kids each had a parent with them, and there was a free-lance photographer/writer doing a story on the boy.

The first few hours were filled with paperwork, films, and lectures, including an explanation of the "quick-learning theory," by which we humans were to learn in two weeks all the trainers had spent six to twelve months teaching the dogs: there would be no discussion or argument; we would be shown what to do and we were to do it. We would get no praise or feedback from the trainers. I didn't realize the implications at the time—how much I need and want encouragement in new, stressful situations. I was too busy thinking about the dogs. I wanted to see them. I began to wonder if they were even in the building—I hadn't heard them bark. But maybe such highly trained dogs didn't bark.

Finally we were escorted into the large back room. We sat in a semicircle facing the two trainers and their assistant. "We're going to bring the dogs in now. You are to ignore them. This is the first time they've been to this building, and they need time to explore it and get used to the new smells. So remember, you are not to touch them or talk to them. If they come up to you, don't respond. We have a lot to cover this morning, so pay attention to us."

The trainers disappeared through a door while we participants sat rigidly quiet. I heard barking! And then the dogs were led in, wearing those beautiful blue and yellow backpacks and leashes—seven golden retrievers, one yellow and two black labrador retrievers. I gasped excitedly and received a critical stare from one of the trainers. The dogs were turned loose. They rushed past us into the next room. It was hard to concentrate on the lecture when I could hear them cavorting behind us. Occasionally, one or two would come and sniff us. When one participant chuckled, the trainer bellowed, "You are not to respond to the dogs! If you can't follow simple instructions, how can we trust you to handle complicated ones when you start working with the dogs!"

Our first practice session would come after lunch. I couldn't wait—I believed these wonderfully trained dogs would do anything I asked. I thought if I said, "Go in the bedroom and look in the third drawer and get my knee socks," the dog would do it.

Was I wrong! We humans quickly discovered that the dogs wouldn't do a single thing we asked. Canines naturally live in packs and develop their own hierarchy based on the animals' leadership qualities. As new members to this pack, we humans had not yet earned any status with these dogs. For the last six to twelve months the trainers had fed, groomed, bathed, played with, and trained the dogs. The dogs saw the trainers as pack leaders, and us as bumbling intruders.

For two days, the trainers stood in the center of our training room and barked commands at us. Our job was to get the dogs to perform the commanded task—"heel," "sit," "down," "stay," and so on. We could use only our voices to encourage the dogs— never the choke collars they wore. We rotated dogs every fifteen minutes. Each time I felt that a dog just might start looking at me, listen to my command and do what I wanted, it was time to trade off for a different dog.

And, Wallaby had indeed been the worst. She had totally ignored me. I had petted her, smiled, cooed, tried different commands, different body movements, and different voice tones. But nothing had worked. I had been grateful that only once in the two days was she rotated to me. In fact, all the dogs were slow to respond to all of us—except Ontario. He had been magnificent, had done everything I asked. (We later learned he was a demonstration dog.) The other goldens had also at least looked at me, and all of them loved to be petted and had kissed me in return. Even the black labs enjoyed being touched. But not Wallaby. No matter who she was with, she would position herself so she could see the trainers, then stare longingly at them. At their slightest recognition, she would wag her tail and grin.

Yet here we were, at the start of the third day, being paired; made a team. I wanted to feel excited. Happy. Secure. But I didn't. I was physically exhausted from the two previous long training days. I was mentally exhausted from the stress of being asked to make so many changes in my feelings about training dogs—especially about correcting them, for this method differed from the one I knew. With these dogs, only praise and positive reinforcement were used. The trainers disciplined themselves— and expected us also—to show no disappointment, frustration, or anger with the dogs and never to scold them.

The training room was always cold. I became chilled, my muscles spasmed and hurt. I missed my heated waterbed and daily whirlpool therapy. I'm a vegetarian, and I missed my regular health-food diet. I missed my husband. I was far more homesick than I wanted to admit. And all the while I was being scrutinized to determine my character and worthiness to receive a CCI dog.

Naturally a positive person, I decided I must make the best of this situation. I said a quick private prayer for strength and set to work. I already felt great respect for the trainers. I was awed by their ability to remain unemotional when correcting the dogs. Yet their love and respect for the animals showed every time they demonstrated a new command. And they wanted all of us to succeed. So I put my trust in their decision that Wallaby was the best dog for me ("You have the skill and personality to give her what she needs") and my heart into winning Wallaby's confidence. I made myself relax.

Wallaby began to respond to me. She was still the slowest to react to commands, but at least she eventually did what I asked. During our lunch break, I retreated to a corner to get to know her. She was beautiful. Technically a yellow lab, her coarse fur was almost white. She had a cinnamon and black nose and honey-colored velvet ears. And big, big, deep brown eyes that seemed to search my blue ones for reassurance. Spontaneously, I reached out and hugged her neck and whispered in her soft ear, "Oh Wallaby! I love you and I want us to be best friends." She squirmed as though uncomfortable with my affection. Feeling hurt, I backed off to just stroking her.

By the end of the day, I truly liked Wallaby. I could tell she wanted to do what I asked but couldn't always understand my unskilled attempts to communicate. I began to discover what motivated her. She responded well to lots of verbal encouragement and praise. She began to watch my face whenever I spoke. When it was time to go back to our motel rooms, I didn't want to leave her.

By the end of the next day, I had earned the right to take her back to the motel with me. The trainers gave me a supply kit for Wallaby with food and water bowls, brush, toothbrush and toothpaste, a pooper scooper, and a twenty-five-pound bag of food. They assisted me in loading her into my van and made sure I could do this safely on my own. I would be totally responsible for her. I felt excited. And scared.

Driving was the only time for the next month (Boot Camp plus our first two weeks at home) that Wallaby and I would not wear our "umbilical" leash. I learned to shower, floss my teeth, dress, eat, and sleep with ninety pounds of (often wiggling) love attached to my left wrist. This constant togetherness, we were told, was necessary to create the bond vital for our working relationship, but sometimes it was awkward. I worried and doubted—Wallaby was supposed to make things easier, not slow me down even more. Then I'd look at her, and she'd wag her tail and wiggle and grin that open-mouthed you're-fun-to-be-with grin, and I'd melt. She learned to lie quietly when I was occupied with something else. She learned I could understand and meet her needs. I fed, watered, and walked her. I brushed her fur and teeth. I bathed and dried her. All the time talking to her, building our private vocabulary, using those trigger words and special looks and touches that would make us truly partners.

Within two days, I knew her "I need to go out" and "I want to play" expressions. She learned "walk" meant we'd go outside, "Are you hungry?" meant I'd feed her, and "cookie" meant I'd give her a treat. At the end of our long training days, we'd go back to our room and I'd take off her backpack and give her the verbal command that let her know she was off duty. Then it was her turn to choose what we'd do. Sometimes she wanted to play with the tennis ball I'd bought her. Sometimes she wanted to chew on her nylabone. Sometimes she'd roll over on her back, wiggling and kicking, begging for a tummy rub. I'd stroke her belly and she'd begin to hum. Yes, hum! Glorious music that made me giggle. Something I realized I hadn't done for a long time.

On our twice daily walks around the motel, I felt less vulnerable. Once a stranger abruptly appeared from between two parked cars and startled me. Wallaby growled so fiercely, I looked to see if another dog had joined us. I felt protected and safe as I hadn't since I started using my wheelchair. She still refuses to "speak" or "guard" on command; but whenever I've been frightened or felt threatened, she growls a warning, "This is *my* person and you better not bother her!"

We blossomed in practice sessions. The better Wallaby responded, the more confident and skilled I became at working with her. I knew we'd make it when, one day, a trainer asked to "borrow" Wallaby to demonstrate a command, and she didn't want to leave me. We advanced to field trips to shopping malls, movie theaters, restaurants, supermarkets, and the zoo. She responded perfectly to all my commands, and I beamed like a proud parent.

The whole class improved. We began to advise, encourage, and support each other—at first just for survival, later out of friendship. The trainers became more relaxed with us, even sometimes praised us. When we couldn't figure out a new task with our dogs, they no longer left us to puzzle it out alone but offered suggestions. We began to have fun.

Our progress was not without setbacks, however. On our first outing—to a big shopping mall—we had all walked our dogs after lunch. Wallaby responded dutifully to the "Better go now" command and I confidently took her back inside the mall. As we headed toward our next destination, I felt her lagging behind. When I turned to investigate, I learned Wallaby can be a walking pooper. I was ashamed! Not that my dog had had an accident; but that I had not read her well and brought her indoors before she was ready. Yet, I learned I could (alone) clean up the mess, using one of the poop-scoop kits she always carries in her backpack. I was an independent new Mom!

As our final exam and graduation approached, I began to tell Wallaby about the other members of her new family/pack. My husband, Jim, flew up for our graduation and the long drive back to Virginia. And waiting at home for us was her brother, an eight-year-old Shih Tzu, Brisbane.

For our first two weeks at home, no human other than me was to talk to, pet, or even look at Wallaby—to ensure that she learned that she was to respond only to me. And she needed to know that I could still meet her needs and keep her safe. Before I had applied to CCI, Jim and I discussed the type of relationship I wanted and expected to have with my service dog. He knew she would in many ways become my most intimate companion. I was relieved when he admitted he might feel some jealousy over this, because then we could talk it out. He has accepted that for her to successfully carry out her work of helping me with my physical needs, she and I needed to have that bond.

Brisbane, too, has adjusted well. Though there is certainly some "sibling rivalry," they are good buddies. Wallaby is gentle with him—she outweighs him by seventy pounds. They play tug with an old knee sock and tag in the fenced yard. Wallaby misses Brisbane when he goes for a haircut or Jim takes him out for a jog. And Jim tells me that Brisbane seems to miss Wallaby whenever she and I go out.

It's been five months since Wallaby and I graduated. I had wondered if when the novelty wore off, I'd feel differently about her. I do. The bond between us is stronger than I had dreamed. We don't wear our leash at home, but we're always together. We've each become an extension of the other; we're uncomfortable apart. Not that we're always within two feet of each other, but we are always close. When I return from one of those rare moments when I'm out of her sight, and she literally leaps into the air, my self-esteem just soars!

She still makes me giggle—sometimes laugh out loud. In public. Like the time I was hurrying through the mall to get some errands done before going to my evening class. All of a sudden Wallaby just stopped. When I looked around, there she was, nose against a shop window, eye-to-eye with a Kermit hand puppet. Her tail wagging, open mouth grinning.

Once I did disappoint her. It was a dark, stormy evening, and Wallaby indicated she needed to go out. I asked her to wait, explaining that it was pouring. She insisted. I put her raincoat on her so I wouldn't have to dry her fur, and opened the door. I've never seen it rain harder. She looked out into the rain and turned her face up to me. Her expression said, "Okay, Mom. Cute. Now turn it off so I can go out." I just laughed. Truly she thought I was all-powerful.

Another time I truly failed her. We were strolling with Jim and Brisbane. I knew a neighborhood dog that sometimes taunted Wallaby had again teased her on our way down the lane, but I hadn't seen the dog on our way back. We stopped to chat with a neighbor. I was inattentive to my dog. That bully dog sneaked up behind us and startled Wallaby into lunging away from me. My arm jerked backward and my scooter flipped, dumping me on the ground. Wallaby immediately returned to my side, obviously distressed. My only physical injury was a minor headache, but I felt awful. My dog had felt threatened, and I had failed to notice. I've since become much more sensitive: what has always gone down the leash is now beginning to flow back up to me.

Wallaby never sees my wheelchair or braces as anything but normal. She continues to thrive on doing what she's been trained to do—to meet my physical limitations with her abilities. It feels somehow that our lives are more complete.

But the big surprise is that *she* motivates *me*. On those tough days when I'm just tempted to stay in my warm bed, she wakes me with kisses and cuddles. She makes it fun to get up. She gives me a sense of purpose.

It's been hard to cope with losing my career. Though I'm back in school, training to be a social worker from my chair, I miss the "giving" part of nursing. Wallaby needs me to give to her. She lifts me not only physically, but spiritually.

There is no greater gift.

Leaving
Dorland Mountain
Alison Townsend

I have before seen other countries, in the same manner, give themselves to you when you are about to leave them, but I had forgotten what it meant. —Isak Dinesen

O n the last night,
　　when I do not dare to hope
that I might see them again,
they come to me, the beautiful
mother and her long-legged daughter,
drifting into the clearing
in coats of tawny smoke.
When I put my book down,
blow the final lamp out and pad,
barefoot through the kitchen
for a glass of cold water,
I see them, lying down together
on the rough grass outside
my window, like two dreams
kneeling on a carpet
of finely woven light.

The moon is everywhere.
Almost full on this warm night,
rising above oak trees in a brief
swell of abandon before autumn,
she shows them to me—
whom I have seen by day
but must meet in another

way before leaving—
this pair who just browse there
beside me with no purpose
but pleasure, moon-bathing
and waiting among the chirr
of crickets and murmurous
hoots of the horned owl,
resting, but not asleep.

They are so close I can see
their flanks moving, each breath
rippling like water beneath the ribs.
I can see their ears, translucent
as furred shells, flick at sounds
I do not notice, and feel their gaze,
lambent as the night itself,
turned deeply upon me,
until the window melts
and there is nothing between us
but breathing measured
by the moon's slow pulse.

The forest heaves
within my body, completely herself
in the guise of these lithe,
delicate women who come to say
that she will take me.
The reward for silence
and attention is acceptance.
The moon will do the rest.

And as I watch, the doe
begins to lick the daughter's face
softly, so softly, I can almost
feel her tongue caress
my pale cheek into
russet velvet layered
over wands of slender bone.
All I want to do

is to lie down there beside them,
slipping free of this tight skin
and letting that wild mother
lick me and tongue me and
polish me into a new life
that curls, glistening and raw
as any naked creature
brought to birth from darkness
and baptized by the moon.

I want to go out there.
But because I want to keep them
this way; because the sound of my
foot on a loose board alarms them;
because I have been permitted
entrance into a secret world, I don't.

I just stand here, for a long time
drinking cold water
and watching, while the deer
watch beside me.

The forest holds me.
And holds me.

In the hushed, nearly imperceptible
pause that comes between each breath
I am her daughter,
innocent again and almost holy.

I have never felt so safe.

III.

Sing to me the
howl of resistance.
Dream to me the forests
of your heart.

A Chicken's Tale in Three Voices
Janet E. Aalfs

I. The Girl

The girl squeezes a white chicken below its flapping wings, breathing hard. The chicken is strong, and certain, until this moment, of freedom. A chopping block stands bloody in the middle of the dusty yard. Chickens peck around it, oblivious to their fate.

The girl wants dinner, a life of her own, shining skin. She stretches the chicken's scrawny neck across the block and holds tight. Her father slices the air, then the chicken, in two. Head and body separate, both still warm. Blood runs over her hands. She opens her clenched eyes, her gripping fingers, and the struggling chicken body falls, feet scratching the air, a thump in the dirt. She clasps her hands behind her back and bleeds. The blood is inside her. The blood is on her hands. *Where do I hide,* she wonders, *from all this death?*

Chicken boils in a pot. The girl has plucked it clean of feathers, her fingers raw. Feathers decorate the edge of her mirror. When she looks at herself, she holds her hand over her throat, feeling for scars. Her mother says, "Why do you collect dust, dirty girl. Girl with no eyes. Take your hand off your mouth. Look at the future. Clean your mirror and decorate your face instead. You'll need it."

When not one more feather can fit in the frame of her mirror, she stores them in boxes under her bed. Her brother holds his nose when he enters her room. Her father sinks his teeth into a thigh and rips the flesh, grease dripping down his chin. Her mother says, "You're driving them away with your hollow eyes. Where is your voice? Why do you shake when they knock?" The girl does not have an answer. She wants dinner. She wants marriage. She has to kill for both.

She saves the feathers for her marriage bed. *A soft one*, she thinks. *One chicken followed by another, then dead. At least there's fate to rely on, a certainty I cannot bemoan.* "I'll kill them myself," her father announces, noticing his daughter's red eyes. He does not want her covered with blood. She is his daughter and she is clean. "Sit on the porch and wait for them. Smile when they come. Look your age."

Her hands dig into flesh. She wants to see bone, sharp in the light. She rolls on her hard mattress above a cloud of feathers and makes herself moan. *My heart is a tortured fish snagged by a hook with no name.* She would not have chosen this body. Too soft. Too many holes. Bumpy skin. Her face is not made to smile. She has rocks in her cheeks and damp armpits. Smells escape from every dark exit. No explanations. Every cell with the same instructions, constantly dying.

"You're wasting a perfectly good life," her mother scolds, waiting for the weather to change to hang the laundry. She had wanted marriage once. It took hard work to find and harder work to get used to. "No one likes a woman who smells like chicken shit."

I won't go forward or backward, the girl thinks, stopping time with her fingers. She sticks them in every opening she can find. The clock stops ticking, the pot stops boiling, her breath stops, her heart.

It is not her fault.

The men come. They tilt their noses up, sniffing. They sit at the table and chat about foxes and other marauders. The girl watches time pass. She sees their mouths move and hears their voices. After dinner, they go away, leaving clouds of dust where their tires spin. Her mother says, "Beggars can't choose what they don't own." Her father says, "She who hides a chicken under the bed will draw the fox." Her brother finds a woman, some children, a house. The girl is not a girl anymore.

The woman still wants dinner but marriage has become a blur. No man can stand the way she smells, and her skin is dull. Her mother says, "You've made your bed, now lie in it." Her father pulls his hair and cries, "How could I have known that raising chickens would lead to this?" The woman who is not a girl anymore laughs. "I owe my life to the chickens we eat. As for the men who pass through this door, they are nothing to me." Her parents throw up their hands in disgust. "Clean out your ears and listen to this!" they bellow. "Chicken shit is no excuse! If you want to be a chicken, go live in the coop." And they kick her out of the house.

The girl who is now a woman flaps her arms and sticks out her neck, cackling wildly as she flies through the front gate into the road. Back in the shrinking doorway, her parents wag their fingers and yell, "Chicken shit!" The chopping block stands empty in the middle of the yard where the chickens scratch furiously, driving their beaks into the rotting wood.

2. The Chopping Block

On my head drips the blood of thousands. Daily. Soaking my pores with its iron stench. I have come to accept my part in nature's design but not without question.

I was a tree once. A living, breathing creature. I stood in a forest surrounded by other plants, and we spoke to each other about the odd ones with legs. It was strange to us the way their trunks split halfway down and became two, disconnected from the ground.

The first time I ever saw one, I didn't know whether to laugh or cry. *How painful,* I thought, *to tear yourself away from the earth with every slight breeze or passing desire. How silly they look, and stiff, in pieces instead of whole.*

I became old and died. The others mourned me as I disintegrated, thankful for all that I gave them even as I passed on. Many winged creatures sat on my naked limbs, and crawly creatures bored into my flesh. I was not alone.

I could have gone on disappearing in this fashion until I was nothing but a memory. Then I would not be here as you see me today, steaming with the spirits of those departed. I used to wish for a different future but found these thoughts tiring after a while.

The legged creature who stole me from the woods was one I had seen before. He carried a metal stick and wore red. The metal stick shot metal rocks into the air with loud explosions. He froze the furry creatures in their tracks and carried them away.

Now I am separate too. He chopped off my limbs to make fire and saved the lowest chunk of my torso. My roots still call to me sometimes, wondering how I'm faring. On good days, I gather all my cells together and rumble. But most times all I can do is sigh.

Don't get me wrong. I'm not regretting my position. Everyone has to have a purpose and this is mine. You must understand, I do not condone what happens on my head. I am a shell of my former self and, as such, have few options.

There is one thing of which I am proud and which makes this existence tolerable. I hold regular counsel with the tunneling creatures who inhabit me. I give them food and they give me information from the underground world. In this way, I keep in touch with the happenings of the earth and do not mourn my roots so.

I have to say life is different now that the girl is gone. Less blood. Fewer headaches from the ring of the axe and the squawking. But I am left with the fury of the pecking creatures and wish they would not take it out on me. They taste the blood of their sisters in my marrow. But it has become a part of me, and I cannot give it back.

3. The Chicken

I come from the open fields to this so-called civilized town to speak to the more liberal-minded among you. I have a favor to ask, but I'll save it until later. I am risking my neck, pardon the expression, and, being no fool, I have taken precautions. If I do not return to my flock, innocent humans may lose their eyes. You've all, I'm sure, seen the movie "The Birds." I need not say more on that account.

Let's face it, it's dangerous to be a chicken in this world. I'm not talking about a scaredy cat but a real live barnyard type. I suppose you think you know me, but don't flatter yourselves. To my sisters it's "Chicken," to you, "Ms. Prairie Hen." Now that I've introduced myself, let me get on with my story.

I stand before you in my golden years, fully aware that I am unusual, mostly because of my age. The only other old chickens I've met are either pets or locked up in zoos. A free old chicken is a rarity indeed. Consequently, we have an incomplete sense of our history. What makes my story unique is that I am alive and free to tell it to you. You may not believe a word of it, and by the time you sit down to dinner tomorrow, you may have forgotten the whole thing. But someday you will look down at your plate and realize that you become what you consume. You will wonder where that drumstick came from, not that you shouldn't eat it, just that you should know.

I was born in a coop and lived there, with no idea about the world beyond, until my escape. Every day was the same, no surprises. The girl scattered corn, we ate it, the sun rose and set, days passed. I was young then, we all were, and innocent, though certainly not oblivious. You'd think we would have been able to imagine more, to realize what was happening. But the mind has a way of protecting even the most savvy from debilitating stress. I know what you featherless ones say—"scattered like a chicken," "running around like a chicken with its head cut off," "Chicken-brain"—all meant to put us down and keep us in our place, pecking in the dirt, lining our nest with feathers, laying eggs. Let me put the evidence on the table: corn on the ground longer than usual, vacant boxes in the coop, a hyperenergetic rooster who would not take no for an answer. And, as if that weren't enough, the girl. She had come with corn in her apron every day since she was tall enough to reach the latch on the gate. She called us each by name as she flung our feed. I was amazed that a human could distinguish us one from the other, not that we looked so much alike, but that she would take the time to notice. She sang to us and spoke in her language. We understood each other well. One day, the girl seemed distracted and did not sing. After about a week, she began mumbling to herself and forgot to call our names. Finally, she made no sound at all. By that time, I had begun to notice other signs of stress. She stopped looking directly at us. The skin on her body became raw where she rubbed and scratched herself incessantly. She stayed no longer than she had to and left quickly without saying good-bye.

Then my sister disappeared. We had shared the same nest and pecked our way out of our shells on the same day. I always knew where she was, even if we were too far away to hear each other's cackling. The morning I noticed her missing was gray and foggy. The girl materialized through the mist in a long cloak with the corn slung in a burlap bag over her shoulder. She didn't bother to scatter our feed but dumped it in a pile at her feet. Then she looked slowly around before lunging in one quick motion toward a little black-and-white-spotted hen that scuttled away out of her reach. I was used to her chasing us in play, and I did not recognize the seriousness of this new game. She cornered a blue beauty at the far edge of the yard where we didn't usually go, pounced, grabbed the unsuspecting creature around the middle, and stuffed her into the bag, pulling the strings tight. The rooster took advantage of our anxious state, mounting first one of us and then another, until we were all dizzy from squawking. I finally managed to make it back to my nest and lay a couple of eggs, hoping these would not be taken, so I would have an excuse to rest for a while, keeping them warm. The girl appeared in the doorway, casting her shadow over me. Without any warning, she snatched me up off my eggs, stranding them to grow cold and die, and squeezed me tightly under her arm to bar my escape. I tried to scratch my way out but her thick cloak and gloves protected her.

She carried me out of that yard and into another, beyond the big red maple, where I had never been. There lay my own sister, her neck stretched across an old stump, in the process of being beheaded. I had never known, thank the Great Fowl Above, that a chicken really does run around without a head until the body, realizing it has lost its sensory connections, drops dead. I can not forgive the girl for allowing me to witness this atrocity. The least she could have done was to throw me in a bag, as she had the others, to spare me the gory details. But this omission on her part was what ultimately saved me, and hence, what allows me to tell you my tale. In her own dismay at what she was seeing, she loosened her grip a fraction. They say chickens can't fly, but I found strength in my wings that I never would have known I had. I flapped wildly, and the girl chased me. She probably would have caught me if she'd kept running. I hopped the fence in the front yard with ease, much to my amazement, and sped across the road into some high grass where I crouched low, barely breathing. I waited, but no one came.

When it got dark, I returned to the coop to tell the others what had happened. They didn't believe me at first. I showed them how I'd used my wings to lift me over the fence. They tried it. They each began to flap, first slowly and with effort, then faster and faster, until the sound of their wings filled the air. I raised my voice above the din, calling "Sisters! Sisters!" They sobered and became silent. One of the oldest chickens said, "We have to act together." I nodded my head in agreement. The yard no longer felt like home, though I had spent my whole life there. I was furious with the girl for betraying us, but I also felt a strange gratitude, for it was she who had inspired me to use my wings. As quietly as we could, we gathered our energy and lifted in a cloud of feathers over the chicken wire and out to freedom.

You can imagine my surprise when, the very next day, from our hiding places in the field, we saw the girl fly out of the house and through the front gate, waving her arms, her eyes ablaze. I wanted to laugh, but I kept my beak tightly closed. For a moment, I felt as sorry for her as I did for myself, looking so wild and crazy, like she wanted to jump out of her skin. Then my fear returned. I realized that something had changed forever. Just as she could never go back there, neither could we. The only thing left to do was to make sure that what had been secret would never be secret again, no matter what our fate proved to be. We vowed to station ourselves in the fields around the house. Every night two of us would fly into the yard and hold counsel with the new batch of chickens. Some of them believed our story and came with us. Others we could not convince. We did our best.

I used to have only nightmares, on the nights when I had time to sleep, and would wake with my head throbbing, crying for my sister. Then this dream:

The girl is a woman with shining skin. She lives in a converted chicken coop with a friend. I am standing at the gate to her yard when she emerges. It is early morning. She stretches her arms over her head, shirt pulled across her breasts. The other woman stands behind and reaches her arms around the girl's middle, hugging her close. They sway back and forth in the sunlight, eyes closed, the picture of bliss. I want to disappear, but I cannot move, transfixed by their beauty. When the girl opens her eyes, she sees me and stops dancing. It is the same split second of shock that allowed me to escape many years before. But this time my life is mine, and I realize I have nothing to fear. She recovers and calls my name. I walk into her yard and up the path. Instead of growing larger the closer I get, the two humans shrink, sprouting feathers all the while. By the time I reach them, it is my sister and another chicken who stand before me.

I woke myself up cackling with joy, the sun already shining, the dream clear in my mind. My fear had dissolved in the night, and my heart was calm. Does anyone here know what became of that girl?

Roja and Leopold
Sally Miller Gearhart

O nce upon a time, in a bedroom community of Silicon Valley, there lived a career woman who was just beginning to make her way in the business world. Through her meditation, her chanting, her networking, and her hard work, she had manifested for herself many friends, many acquaintances, and scores of contacts. Her name was Constance.

Constance no longer had a husband, for he had deserted her years before when she was more vulnerable and less murderous. Her job paid better every year. Her social life was that of a very swinging single. Every day she felt herself growing wiser, more experienced. Her learning curve was steep, her savvy increased in direct proportion to her ambition, and she was stashing away every other paycheck in flexible mutual funds.

However, Constance did have two crosses to bear. One was her daughter, a strong, independent little girl whom we shall call Roja. Roja was a cross to her mother because a) Constance had never wanted children—she had borne Roja because her sensitivity group had helped her uncover deeply buried (and unfortunately very temporary) maternal feelings—and b) Roja didn't give a tinker's damn for Constance either, wishing only to spend her time with her girlfriend or her grandmother, both of whom could think laterally and had alternative views of everything, from consumerism and politics to lifestyle and religion.

Constance's second cross was Roja's grandmother, known as Geraldine to all her bridge and skydiving partners and to the small band of subversive activists who met weekly to plot the liberation of abused nonhuman animals. Geraldine was a burden to Constance because she was dying of cancer. Geraldine knew she was dying, had said her good-byes to the world, and was ready to go. Constance, however, felt it her duty to consult with doctors, who kept coming up with miraculous new life-prolonging drugs and surgical techniques.

All Geraldine wanted to do was die, preferably at the hands of a large ferocious tiger so the animal nations could get back some of the meat they had been providing humans for so long. And all Constance wanted to do was keep her conscience clear so nobody could say she hadn't tried everything to save her mother. All the doctors wanted to do was practice more heroic measures on Geraldine's body.

So, in her tiny house in the great forest that bordered her daughter's condominium, Geraldine lived on, long past her desire to do so. She was under the care of a top-of-the-line robot nurse whose switch she managed to keep on "Off" most of the time and whose mechanism she was constantly manipulating in the vain effort to heist some barbiturates or commandeer a razor blade.

But Geraldine had never been simply a single-issue activist, nor was she now, well into her nineties. And so, though she constantly scoured the premises for the available means of suicide, she also searched diligently for clues to a great universal healing that she was convinced lurked just beneath the surface of every violet petal, just under the reflection on the back of every puddle in the sun, just between the cracks in the wooden floor, or in the interstices between the spider's web and the dust motes that it sifted. She called the object of her search the "Fallen Threads," or whatever-it-was-that-had-once-held-things-together-in-a-kind-of-empathy-or-mutual-understanding.

She had dreams about broken paths, dammed-up or disconnected rivers, chain ends lying limp for lack of a link, gold rings with a segment of themselves removed, but most of all she dreamed of tattered strings of cotton and wool that swayed in the breeze and reached across an abyss in the effort to weave together again with partner wisps that were swaying and reaching from the other side. Sometimes they touched, sometimes even strained beyond to fold themselves together in the genesis of a slender strand, only to be torn apart once more.

Sometimes, in her waking hours, Geraldine could feel the presence of the lost Threads. Sometimes when she breathed with the frog or swooped with the housefly, she seemed to fall into a pocket of their presence, where she was surrounded by them and they called to her. "Here we are! Just over here!" Her eyes could never move fast enough and her touch was always too clumsy. She could not catch them, and when she tried, she was catapulted out of the pocket. The best she could do was listen.

And then she could feel the Threads at work, reaching and binding, twining and winding, almost mending a break, almost reweaving a strand, then ... Snap! They were gone, broken again. Forced apart by some coolness, some distancing, an interference, a consciousness somewhere that stepped between the doer and the done-to, between the tool and that which was to be changed by the tool.

So Geraldine kept looking for the Threads, opening herself to the creatures in whose presence those Threads seemed to dwell, trying to learn to be very still and listen. She listened while the Threads struggled to reweave themselves into a tiny fragment of a tapestry severed from itself.

Thus you could see the old woman most any time of day or night, standing stock still by her window. You'd never guess she was slipping inside the skin of a wandering vole or a tall-eared jackbunny. Or sometimes she would be examining the snail slime on a hollyhock bloom or squatting under the dewdrops on the pea vines or scrutinizing splinters of starlight and muttering, "I wonder if that's them?" The only one who ever helped her look for the Threads was her buddy, Roja, who would visit every week or so. The two of them, listening together, could sit smack-dab in the middle of a sow bug and take up no room at all. And there they could feel the Threads at work, feel them reaching and weaving. She was a good one, that girl. Better than her mother. Nature's always best skipping a generation, Geraldine decided.

Geraldine's daughter Constance, to her credit, was never hypocritical about the vast distances that separated her from her mother. Instead of visiting Geraldine herself, she had early on adopted the custom of sending gifts of fancy (and some pretty degenerate) edibles to the old woman. Every Sunday she packed up a wonderful basket of finger foods, breads, chips, dips, nuts, Hostess Ho-Hos and other sweets, all to be carried through the woods by Roja. This ritual served two purposes for Constance: Grandma Geraldine got a gift of filial affection, and the kid was out of her hair for a whole night. Constance usually went to a singles' bar and cruised.

Roja loved to visit her grandmother. The hike itself was a healthy one, filled with flowers, trees, birds, and breezes that often conspired to delay her until sunset. Further, she loved Geraldine herself, the songs they sang, the Threads they searched for, the games they played with n-dimensional analysis and word jumbles and the *Wall Street Journal*. Then, after tucking in the old woman for a sweet sleep, she would skip her way further into the forest to stay overnight with her friend and lover, Ermendina, who lived and worked and had her being just a bit beyond Grandma's house.

One Sunday at high noon, burdened only by her jam-packed, food-filled, North Face rucksack, Roja skipped her way to Grandma's house, humming one of those heavy-metal ditties and thinking about her girlfriend, Ermendina, who was working day shift at the hospital. She wasn't paying much attention to the path and was surprised when a large figure suddenly loomed before her.

Now this large figure was none other than Leopold the Wolf, actually the most unhappy wolf in the whole consolidated pack that roamed the streets and parks of Silicon Valley. Leopold was unhappy because he was a closet vegetarian. The thought of devouring flesh repelled him.

Fully aware that the unexamined life is not worth living, he had long ago conducted a careful self-analysis of his family constellation and his early puphood in the effort to locate the cause of his abnormality. He now knew that his vegetarianism stemmed from the circumstances of his first home in the north where he, the last-weaned of his sisters and brothers, had been orphaned to the care of one of the tundra's most highly sophisticated wolf packs, a pack that had eschewed the nomadic life and the insecurity of the immediate kill and opted instead for a fixed pastoral society. In this case, the pack had rapidly reached that dangerous stage in any society's development when it needs must deal with the storage of surplus flesh.

And Leopold had seen for himself the atrocities of those factory farms. Though he had been but a pup, he had been sickened by the sight of those captured and imprisoned animals, and particularly the human animals, all being fattened for the pack's food. He was particularly sensitive to the humans because he had had one for a pet until it was slaughtered at the age of two. In fact, the only thing worse for him than the sight of the humans so cramped together there in the enlarged warrens, unable to move, had been his witness of their ultimate slaughter.

He was deeply troubled by his internal contradictions. He believed in Nature, Red In Tooth And Claw, believed in the necessity of the chase and the hunt, believed these things to be inherent in wolf being. But the pack's cruelty in this mass imprisonment and slaughter of beings so much like himself seemed an unnecessary indignity, an abrogation of rights, an atrocity. He recalled vividly how in protest he nearly starved until he discovered that he could be nourished, as many other animals were, by prairie grass and meadow fronds.

Secretly, he was glad when that renegade pastoral society had failed and he and friends had made their perilous way south. But Leopold never forgot his months on the tundra, and the memory of those months rendered even hunting impossible for him. He had lived since then as an imposter, under a thin veil of hypocrisy. But at least, he reminded himself, his honor was untarnished, his escutcheon unblemished, for in his heart he was at peace as a vegetarian. He had made his pact with the nations of the Earthfreed, swearing never to take the lives of their members, and with the nations of the Earthbound, thanking them for their provision of his sustenance and always revering them.

Still, Leopold the Wolf had to spend extensive time foraging for food and learning to grind herbs and berries between his large canine teeth. He spent, it seemed, the remainder of his time concealing his abnormality from other wolves, becoming a master storyteller over the years as he deflected inquiries about where he had been and why he never appeared to have any fresh blood dripping from his muzzle.

On this sunny day in the Silicon Valley Forest, his secret was perilously close to being discovered by his pack, because by this time they knew him well, and since they were animals of long and appreciative memory, they recalled his every variation on each of the thirty-seven basic plots. He was, very simply, running out of stories. Soon he would have to show evidence that he had Made A Kill. Soon he would have to forsake the fields and gardens where bloomed those tasty essences and behave as a real wolf should, preying upon and devouring, for instance, little girls who skipped alone through the forest.

"And where are you going?" he growled in his deepest voice to Roja.

"Oh!" she said, frightened. "I'm just on my way to Grandma's house to bring her food."

"How wonderfully quaint," breathed Leopold, measuring Roja's throat from a three-quarter angle as he had seen his fellows do. "And, pray, my pretty, where does your grandmother live?" he added, nagged by the suspicion that he was uttering some oft-spoken script.

Roja suddenly felt as if she had fallen into a pocket of Threads. She was somehow in kinship with this great beast, though not identical with him as she and Geraldine sometimes were with the sow bugs. She wanted to fall upon him and stroke him.

Instead she tried to listen to the Threads even as she answered, "Only a mile or so over yonder." Then, because the feeling escaped her and because she felt socially inept, she blurted, "Want to play gin?" She extended the well-worn deck of cards she and Ermendina always carried to music festivals.

Leopold was taken off guard by her offer, and to center himself he did a quick energy-run, concentrating on the yellow chakra. Roja had spread out her hooded cape on the soft earth and was cutting for deal. She pushed a Ho-Ho toward him.

Leopold struggled to take charge of the situation. "No. I don't do gin," he said. "And I thought you were taking that food to your grandmother."

"I am, but she won't care if we eat it. She's dying. Or trying to. If she can keep them from reconnecting her tubes, she thinks she can starve by Solstice."

"Really," said Leopold. He sat tailor-fashion beside the girl, suddenly more interested than ever in pursuing this fortunate encounter. "Tell me about your grandmother," he said, taking a giant swig from the Pepsi Roja offered him.

"Well, I love the old lady a lot," Roja said, munching on chilled beansprouts. "But I wish she could die."

"You want your grandmother to die?" Leopold asked, shocked.

"Ummmmm. She's longing for it and it just won't happen. I'd miss her, of course, but I'd be very happy for her."

And so it went. For the better part of the afternoon, the two strangers shared stories about their families and friends, their hopes and dreams, their self-hatred and their fears, though Leopold resisted telling her of his greatest shame. He revealed instead that he was a seventeenth-century buff, and Roja played some ancient ballads for him on her harmonica. He sang in a soft baritone that charmed not only Roja but the juncos and cardinals as well.

When the sun dropped into late afternoon, Leopold realized he must get on with the task of Making A Kill. And certainly this little girl could not qualify as A Kill. He felt he had established too much connection with her. Perhaps he was even feeling the presence of the Threads she had told him about. Besides, as she talked, a plan had begun to evolve in his mind, a plan so audacious he felt sure he could never carry it off. And yet, he was eager to dare its accomplishment.

He said good-bye to her and assured her they could meet again the next Sunday, though he secretly knew he would be seeing her much sooner than that. He was finding himself quite reluctant to part from her, for they had struck a warm and immediate friendship. His paw touched her hand in a moment of interspecies understanding, and they went their separate ways.

"Friendship, friendship, just a wonderful blendship," sang Roja, as she skipped through the woods with the remnants of her gifts to Grandma. "Reach out and touch someone," sang the wolf, as he raced down the ravine and over the shortcut to Geraldine's house.

Leopold sped straight to Geraldine's bedside where he found her in deep meditation trying unsuccessfully to convince her tenacious heart that it was time to blow this popsicle shop. When he explained that he had come to liberate her from this Vale of Sorrow, Geraldine flung her arms around him and, momentarily confused about her identity, licked his face and panted. The Threads were very close by in that moment. The Threads were, in fact, in an apoplexy of touching and weaving.

Thus the two ruffians schemed together, speedily and gleefully, about how he, Leopold, could ease her, Geraldine, into oblivion and how she, Geraldine, could help him, Leopold, look like a blood-drenched carnivore. They decided that Leopold would pick one of those terrifying woman-in-danger plots that Hitchcock was so good at, condense it for this special occasion, and simply scare Geraldine to death——or exhaust her——with his rendition of it.

"But you got to get my blood now, Sonny, 'cause they tell me it don't flow after you go."

Gentle Leopold was horrified. He shuddered and grew pale. "Now? Now, before—"

"Druantia, deliver me from Sensitive Males!" grumped the old woman. "Now just swipe that syringe from Bessie Bluecross over there," she said, pointing to the inert robot, "and you can drain my venous line into that special tube yonder. 'Twon't hurt me a bit."

It was at that moment that the whole enterprise almost floundered, for Leopold, as we know, had no stomach for blood. But finally, with his hand over his eyes and peeping between claws only enough to get the job done, he did as Geraldine directed. To his undying amazement, the old woman smiled dreamily all the while.

"Take all you need," she urged. "In fact, take a little extra for another day." She began humming a Billie Holiday classic. "This is not a Peak Experience, but it's sure better than I thought it would be."

Leopold triumphed. With blood a-plenty at his disposal, he managed to gather himself together and settled himself on the bed, making as much of a lap as he could for the old woman to sit upon. He wrapped his furry arms about her and rocked her forward and back, around and around, while he spun out an old-fashioned tale of suspense and terror.

As he talked, she found herself more and more aware of the Threads, of their presence below and above her, around and over her. And he did indeed tell a good story, Geraldine decided.

"My friend Lollie would love that part," she murmured, "the part about how the crone decides to take karate." She imagined herself in a crisp white gi with her black belt modestly circling her waist.

"Yes," crooned Leopold, allowing that cue to point his narrative down an unexpected path. "She stayed often at the dojo, even after others had gone home, working in front of the mirror, shaping her ki-flow into whatever weapon she willed it to be. On this particular night, she deliberately planned to stay late because she was part of a cunning trap that the Shirley Temple

Gang was setting for the Wrinkle Killer, the madman who had terrorized them and the city for months now, isolating and murdering old women. This might be the evening when he would fall for their bait. She was ready."

The wolf's voice took on an ominously normal quality. What little blood still rode through Geraldine's veins was chilled to a snail's pace. "It was very late that night," he was saying, "when she went back for one last kata and forty final first-form kicks. Her teacher had called to her as she left, 'Door is locked, Gerry!' and she had called back, 'Thanks!' And now the dojo was quiet."

Geraldine stirred slightly in the arms of the wolf. Her eyes were closed, her heart pumping slow but still strongly. She was filled with an enormous sense of well-being even as she thrilled to the coming of the inevitable. Leopold spoke now sotto voce, barely above a tense whisper. "As she made her precise recovery from her twelfth kick, she thought she caught a flash of movement in the far corner of the wide mirror . . ."

Geraldine's heart sped a little faster. Leopold continued.

"There! There it was again! She disciplined herself to continue the exercise, showing no trace of having noticed. As she extended ki through her high foot she allowed herself a glance at the corner of the mirror. By the door of the dojo, behind her and far to the left, was a long deep shadow that should not have been there. She swallowed and inhaled, pushing protective ki out into her aura."

In Leopold's arms, Geraldine clenched her upright fists and positioned them perpendicular to her body. The wolf's voice grew tense. "She returned her clenched fists to her alert posture and emitted a controlled ki-ay as she delivered her next kick. The shadow was still there, unmoving. When she executed her thirty-fifth kick, she saw that it had disappeared, presumably into the darkened change-room area. 'Be ready, girls!' she muttered toward Mamie Carter and the band of old women that she hoped were waiting in the basement, 'I think we've got our man!'"

Geraldine's heart was pounding now. "What a way to go!" she thought. "Like a hero!" The Threads were right there with her, weaving themselves together with the rhythm of her heart. Her chest rose high and fell low, over and over again as she rested in the embrace of the master raconteur.

He was telling now of the moment in the dressing room when

the woman turned, and the Wrinkle Killer dodged behind a stack of mats. Then, of the moment when she let him know she knew he was pursuing her. The swift rush for the stairs, the running downward, downward, three flights, four flights, down to the first floor and on toward the basement.

"She heard the door above her slam and at that same moment the stairwell was plunged into blackness. She froze. There was no sound, only her own rapid breathing. She pulled in her ki, forcing herself to breathe steadily. Where was he? Was he coming silently through the darkness? Was he only inches away? Then she heard it, the slow shuffle. Once. Twice. High above her. Moving toward her, faster now with his increasingly more certain footing."

Geraldine, tense in Leopold's arms, gasped and emitted a soft cry. She was suddenly aware that she could no longer hear Leopold's words, that she was hearing now the sounds, feeling now the textures, that were in his mind. If there had been light in the stairwell, she would be seeing the pictures in his mind.

The dark figure was chasing her now, her, Geraldine, in a white gi with a black belt, chasing her, Geraldine, down the stairs from the dojo toward the cellar. She stood there on the lightless landing, drawing him toward her, willing him to scuttle faster and faster down the cement steps to where she waited.

She was ready. But not ready enough. She felt rather than saw his leap from the landing just above her, into the air. She lifted her hands in a block, but he landed full-weight upon her, knocking her backward and down the last flight of stairs. A knife-like pain shot through her arm. She forced her knee into a crevice between their bodies and flung him over her head.

Before she was erect on her knees to defend, she took his foot full under her jaw and went reeling against the wall. His fist followed her, lifting her upright as it plunged deep into her nose and cheek. Her head was full of agonizing light. She could hardly breathe, and the thunder of the blood in her ears drowned out her scream. But she had his wrist now at a control angle. He winced. He would be completely at her mercy and literally on his knees the second she chose to put the torque to that flabby wrist joint. She grinned in the darkness, enjoying his grunts and wheezes. She knew his strength, knew her one good hand with that simple wrist torque was all that stood between her and her certain death.

And that reminded her.

She waited until she heard the shouts of the Shirley Temple Gang and the burst of ancient energy that flooded through the basement door. Then she calmly dropped the man's hand and deposited him in the hands of the old women. She hoped he could see her enigmatic smile. She lay back on a thick blanket of Threads.

"Thank you, Leopold!" she whispered and drew her last breath.

Leopold felt the frail bundle that he held in his arms contract into a suddenly closer embrace. He held her close, riding with her on the cradle of Threads. He waited for a long moment. Then he sighed and reverently carried her from the bed to the closet.

Compelled either by the desire to tease Roja, his new-found friend, or by that unarticulable sense of grim mythos he had felt off and on all day, he donned Geraldine's gown and her bedcap and crawled into the her bed, feigning as best he could the demeanor of the old woman. He chuckled as he thought of how much Roja would appreciate this game of impostership. He finally heard her knocking on the cottage door. Clearly she had been dawdling again, visiting with ants and bluebirds while he waited here with this surprise.

"Come in!" he crooned.

Unsuspecting, Roja bounced to the bedside to greet her grandmother. She politely hid her opinion that the old girl was looking quite robust today and instead began hauling out Fritos, dips, and what was left of the Ho-Hos, for their mutual consumption. She was at the point of telling Geraldine about the wonderful wolf she had met in the forest when she noticed the pointed ears emerging from her grandma's nightcap.

"Why Grandma," she said, "what big ears you have!"

"The better to hear you with, my dear," sighed the wolf.

"And Grandma, what big eyes!"

"The better to see you with as well."

"And oh," said Roja, feigning fear, "your teeth! Your teeth, Grandma, are very large! Do such teeth run in the family? Will I have teeth like that when I grow up?"

At that Leopold flung off his costume and stood split naked

on the bed like the righteous self-respecting wolf that he was. "I am not your grandmother!" he shouted.

Roja was stunned, then as she realized what had transpired, delighted. The wolf took her by the hand and led her to Geraldine, and while the two of them dressed the old woman's body in a sheet that looked like a white gi, he explained to Roja all that had happened.

They performed a gentle ritual of gratitude and rejoicing over the body of Geraldine. Then, with immaculate skill and dispatch, they smeared her blood that he had drawn earlier generously all over Leopold, particularly over his paws and chops, until he looked like the fiercest of monster hunters, still digesting his Kill.

In the dusk, the two friends embraced, being careful to keep the blood off Roja's cape, and swore to meet again, not only to renew their ties of kinship but also to provide Leopold with other sources of blood for his charade: Roja's girl friend, Ermendina, knew hundreds of folks eager to find such a quick and easy death. The wolf need never again fear the pressure of his peers, and indeed, he howled like the leader of the pack as he streaked across the parks and freeways to rejoin his kin.

Nearby, a woodsman, unaware of his brush with an alternate destiny, hummed an environmental tune as he dialogued with his trees and reflected upon the sweet sameness of his daily routine.

Roja made things look as if Geraldine had died in her sleep, then kissed her grandmother's cool cheek. She decided it was time to run away from home. She frolicked her way to Ermendina's to embark on a life of increasingly intense love and lust which was later documented by Shere Hite in *The Turn-of-the-Century Report.*

Constance, at last blissfully relieved of both her mother and her daughter, fulfilled the deep longing she had only recently discovered to follow a beautiful guru whose U.S. visit had changed her life. Over the next fifteen years, she sent occasional postcards from India to her daughter and Ermendina.

Everyone, from the juncos in the trees to the peaceful wolf inhaling luscious-smelling berry blossoms in the field behind the shopping mall, lived (and died) happily ever after.

On Looking to Nature for Women's Sphere

Jane Curry

Samantha, the Lord designed it that females should stay to hum and tend to their babies, and wash the dishes. And when you go aginst that idee you are goin' aginst the everlastin' forces of nater. Nater has always had laws sot and immovable, and always will have 'em, and a passel of wimmen managers or lecturers hain't a-goin' to turn 'em round. —Josiah Allen, circa 1873

In different centuries, in different dialects, from flesh-and-blood people and fictional folks, we have heard the arguments that purportedly look to nature for guidance. Josiah Allen, a fictional character created by author Marietta Holley, would no doubt take me for one of those "wimmen lecturers" he disdains. I know him well because I travel throughout the country impersonating Josiah Allen's wife in a one-woman performance called "Samantha Rastles the Woman Question." And I repeatedly see with what head-nodding, frivolity, and chortling triumph audiences greet Josiah's comeuppance with regard to "nater."

In a scene from *My Opinions and Betsey Bobbet's* (1873), Samantha Smith Allen, rustic philosopher and advocate of women's rights, and Horace Greeley, nineteenth-century editor and political leader, discuss the prevailing habit of using nature to justify the assignment of human spheres. In particular, Victorians ceaselessly argued that, as in nature, males should be preeminent in the public sphere, females in the private. Horace claims: "Man is sometimes mistaken in his honest beliefs, but Nature makes her laws unerringly. Nature designed man to be at the head of all public affairs. Nature never makes any mistakes." Samantha counters: "Nature made queen bees, Horace. Old Nature herself clapped the crown on 'em. You never heard of king bees, did you?"

Samantha goes on to describe the "public duties" of the queen bee, whose subjects are up early for work and home "stiddy" at night and whose nation is marked by industrious, "equinomical" housekeeping. Not wanting to appear heartless, Samantha assures Horace that she doesn't approve of one aspect of the hive's operation. If the female bees can't make enough honey to last the entire hive through the entire winter, well, they kill off all the male bees. She doesn't approve of it. She doesn't think those lazy, drone husband bees "ort" to be killed off just to keep from "winterin' 'em." But every law of nature has its little eccentricity, and this is "hern." "But other'n that," says Samantha, "many a man who has sat in high chairs ort to look to the queen bee as a pattern of the Executive Female."

In another declaration of nature's designs, Samantha's husband, Josiah, generalizes about nature's immovable laws and their presumed applicability to human behavior. "In all the works of nater, the females stay to hum, and the males soar out free." On a visit to an ostrich farm, Josiah instructs Samantha to pay attention as the manager describes the habits of the ostriches: "I always love to have a female hear about the works of nater. It has a tendency to keep her in her place." But as it turns out, the female ostrich lays that egg; she surely does, there's not a doubt about it. And for six hours out of every twenty-four, she stays to home, on the nest, incubating the eggs—in the private "spear," as it were. But for the other eighteen hours a day, she wanders in the world, taking charge of public affairs. The male ostrich stays to home, on the nest, incubating the eggs—in the private "spear," as it were. Josiah is "vury" upset at the news.

While the strange spelling, dialect, and unfamiliar syntax of nineteenth-century humor are no longer in fashion, the ideas seem to evaporate for awhile and then come back again like rain. One hundred years after the fictitious Samantha Allen tackled the tenacious nature argument against women's participation as enfranchised citizens of the republic, one still hears that it is natural for females to care for the young, natural that males are stronger and bigger than females, natural that males are aggressive and females passive, et cetera.

It's hardly a new idea to question the selectivity with which "nature" is used to suggest norms of human behavior. Josiah looked to the nature comprised of dogs and cats and such. Samantha preferred bees and ostriches. (Ah, yes, the skeptics will murmur: one group consists of mammals and the other of insects and birds. Well, majoritarians might note that most animal species are insects, but even in the varieties of birds, fishes, reptiles, and mammals there are habits that would have exacerbated Josiah's periodic case of "aperplexy.") So it does seem only natural, so to speak, that if different selections were made as illustrations of nature's laws, the norms would be perceived differently. After all, where, in nature, is it written that the females clean the toilets?

What might we deduce, for example, about the care and feeding of human young if we used penguins as our model? The female lays the egg, and then she takes to sea for two to four months. While she is out to sea, the male incubates the egg, which in many species is held in special abdominal pouches. Males fast during these months, losing a third to a half of their body weight, and feed the young from craw reserves until the female returns. In the largest species, the emperor penguin, the male incubates a single egg on his foot while the female is off getting fat. By the time she returns to take over, his ninety-pound weight has been reduced to approximately forty-five pounds.

Now think of the impact this model would have on architecture, dieting, acrobatics, and postpartum travel, at the very least. Sailors' homes in New England shore towns would all need widower's walks. The starved look would be fashionable among new fathers advocating the Anchorage Rookery Diet. The muscle control and precision movement of males delicately balancing newborns on their feet could lead to a whole new pool of potential Olympic talent. And new mothers need feel no guilt over either extra weight after pregnancy or postpartum wanderlust. Why, it could also affect the spacing of children in a household and hence serve as a birth control strategy. If babies were born too close together, the poor father might not have a chance to bulk up again in between. Naturally, too many births or (gasp) multiple births might see him wasting away literally to nothing.

Actually, if the majoritarians had prevailed in deducing human norms from nature, we would never have hired nannies, opened childcare centers, invented the collapsible stroller, or funded studies on latchkey children. In over ninety-nine percent of animals, the female lays the eggs or gives birth and then takes no further part in their survival. Some form of parental care exists in some species of every major group of animals, but the vast majority show no parental care at all. In those that do, it's not all swaggering pride and pass out the cigars, thank you very much, for the males.

In many bird species, for example, the nest building, incubating, and feeding of the young are shared by the male and female— to wit: parrots, oyster catchers, petrels, snipes, terns, thrashers vultures, woodpeckers, bluebirds, condors, flamingoes, jays, killdeer. In some mouth-brooding fishes (stickleback, Siamese fighting fish) only the males watch over the young until the fry leave their underwater nests.

Only a few snake species incubate or guard the eggs, and none care for the young after they hatch. But some frog fathers take their responsibilities very seriously indeed. Not all frogs come from tadpoles. The female Andean Darwin's frog lays her eggs and returns to the water. The male lingers with a group of his colleagues who have been attracted to the scene. They watch the eggs for several days, and when the eggs are about ready to hatch into tadpoles, each male picks up a number of them and slides them with his tongue deep into his vocal pouch. They remain in the safety of his throat until they crawl out some days later as little frogs. In poison frog species, the male repeatedly visits the eggs left by the female. When, after several weeks, the tadpoles hatch, they crawl aboard the male's back and he carries them to their new home in the pond.

And among mammals, while parental care is generally the rule, there is no one pattern of behavior. Some pairs mate for life (jackals), some are promiscuous (zebras, most whales, chimpanzees). In some species, males and females travel together in herds, packs, or prides (musk-ox, wolves, lions); in others, family groups are the basic unit (coyotes, gibbons); in others, males and females spend most of their time in same-sex groups and get together only for mating (hippopotamuses); in still others, all are loners who seek out members of their species only for the purpose of procreation (pandas). Banded and dwarf mongooses cooperate among themselves to take care of the young—one or two members of the pack clean, feed, and protect the offspring while other adults hunt. All adult wolves help care for all pups. Male marmosets and tamarins carry their young, usually twins, on their backs and may hand the offspring to the mothers only at feeding time. Among wild dogs, both parents care for the young. For most monkeys, the basic social unit is matrilineal. Savannah-dwelling baboons illustrate a system of either "complementary equality" between females and males (a term used by Shirley Strum in *Almost Human: A Journey into the World of Baboons*) or matriarchy.

So what is "normal and natural"? I suppose firstborns should be comforted in the knowledge that we didn't follow the example of dwarf cichlid fish who eat their first brood but not later ones.

And only a sadist would suggest that we look to notable insect species for guides to the regulation of domestic squabbles. Few unproductive husbands meet the fate of the drone bees, legally at least. But those males uncomfortable with female assertiveness in matters sexual could hardly remain poker-faced at the lovemaking prospects. The female scorpion opens by killing the male after mating. The black widow spider ups the ante by eating the male after mating. Then we can raise you a praying mantis: the female may or may not devour the male while they are mating. The kicker here is that as the female eats first his eyes, then his head, and so on, the male becomes ever more amorous. As far as I know, Masters and Johnson have never recommended this technique in their therapies.

Of course, the curious will immediately want to consult Robert A. Wallace's ever helpful guide, *How They Do It*, for details of the copulating habits of everything from snails to seahorses. Snails are hermaphrodites. Earthworms too. Bedbugs are homosexual. Geese indulge in ménages à trois. And seahorses—well, seahorses could give new meaning to that family planning poster showing a man pregnant and asking the logical question, "What would you do if it were you?" Seahorses engage in an elaborate courtship affair which ends when the female deposits up to six hundred eggs into the male's abdominal sac, after which, she swims away with no further responsibility. He releases sperm to fertilize the eggs and settles in for a fifty-day "pregnancy." During that time, the eggs develop and hatch inside the pouch, which is eventually swollen with hundreds of tiny seahorses. When the "pregnancy" is terminated, he suffers repeated spasmodic contractions that expel one or more offspring at a time, until all the violent heaving and wrenching is over. If even one decaying corpse is left in his pouch, he could die. Well, nobody said biological determinism would be easy, now did they?

In fact, you may as well know the truth. Females are larger than males in a majority of species. Even though males are generally larger in mammalian species, a surprising number of families contain species with larger females: twelve of twenty orders and twenty of one hundred and twenty-two families. Good grief, it's getting so you can't take stock in any assumptions anymore. In an article in *Natural History* (June 1982), Stephen Jay Gould discusses the size and function of males and females in the evolutionary schemes of nature. The title may give you a clue: "The Oddball Human Male." He reminds us that "since blue whales are the largest animals that have ever lived, and since females surpass males in baleen whales, the largest individual animal of all time is undoubtedly a female. The largest reliably measured whale was 93.5 feet long and a female." (Dinosaurs may have gotten as long but not as heavy.)

And what's more, the males of some species become dwarfs and evolve into little more than a sperm delivery system. Consider some species of the ceratoid anglerfishes who live up to ten thousand feet below the ocean's surface, where both food and populations are sparse. They serve as nature's answer to the question put after two drinks in a singles' bar, "And are you attached?" The male anglerfish, approximately two inches in length, is literally attached to the female, who is over ten times his size. Their vascular systems are continuous; the male doesn't function as an independent organism. Alas, he has evolved to no more than a sexual appendage of the female, "a kind of incorporated penis." Don't jump to conclusions, though. While it has often seemed in human marriages that man and woman become one, and that one is the man, the male anglerfish is not totally submerged into this oneness of union. He has an identity of his own. It's true that he depends on her for nutrition, that she supplies the blood, that some of his organs are lost or reduced because he has no need of them. But his own heart beats and his own kidneys may remove wastes. He may even be capable of changing his position with movement of tail and fins. Of course, he may also have to tolerate rivals for her vascular affections—several males are often embedded into a single female. But what more freedom could he desire when he's so ably taken care of by the larger, stronger algaewinner?

And then, dare I mention it, there is the matter of the toothcarp of Mexico and Texas and the teiid lizard family of the Americas. These deviants would no doubt force Phyllis Schlafly and Jerry Falwell into a rhetorical frenzy. In the toothcarp, all individuals are female. Males don't exist. Talk about disrupting your traditional family unit. When they mate, females seek out males of a related species and dupe them into donating their sperm. Those sperm, however, don't actually unite with the eggs or contribute their genes to the offspring. Instead the sperm stimulate the eggs to begin their development. This done, the sperm fall uselessly away, carrying their genes with them. Nobody seems to know what happened to the male toothcarps or how they became so totally useless that nature, in "her" ever efficient way, dispatched them to oblivion.

The majority of the two hundred and thirty species of the teiid lizard family are found in South America. Most reproduce by laying eggs, and most must mate first in the usual way. However, in a few unisexual species, no mating is necessary. In these teiids, all individuals are female and can lay eggs which do not need to be fertilized and which hatch into more females. Thus they dispense with the need for males altogether. Clearly the toothcarp and the teiid lizard could drastically alter even Josiah Allen's view of women's place.

Larger females, "pregnant" males, he-fish housekeepers, single-sex species, absent mothers, shared-parenting, killing, maiming, and general mayhem. What's a person to think? These are as much a part of nature as the forms and behaviors we more commonly look to for models.

Of course, looking to nature for women's sphere has often been a self-serving exercise in manipulating the evidence to fit a preconceived conclusion. Or, as Mark Twain, the male Marietta Holley of his day, put it: "There is something fascinating about science. One gets such wholesale returns of conjecture out of such a trifling investment of fact." Here is this month's dividend: who are we to argue with Nature? If we look to nature for models of human behavior, we are bound, are we not, to value tolerance and pluralism.

The Feminist-Vegetarian Quest

Carol J. Adams

We have learned to use anger as we have learned to use the dead flesh of animals, and bruised, battered and changing, we have survived and grown, in Angela's Wilson's words, we are moving on. —Audre Lorde, "The Uses of Anger: Women Responding to Racism"

In her angry feminist novel *Frankenstein*, Mary Wollstonecraft Shelley makes her Monster, who is at odds with its world, a vegetarian. Percy Shelley titled his first vegetarian essay *A Vindication of Natural Diet*, after Mary Wollstonecraft's *A Vindication of the Rights of Woman*, implying the alliance he saw between vegetarianism and feminism. His poem *Queen Mab* envisions a feminist, vegetarian, and pacifist utopia one hundred years before Charlotte Perkins Gilman's *Herland*.

We can find feminism and vegetarianism allied in various historical times—in utopian writings and societies, anti-vivisection activism, the temperance and suffrage movements, and twentieth-century pacifism. Susan B. Anthony, Elizabeth Cady Stanton, Sojourner Truth and others frequented hydropathic institutes which featured vegetarian regimens. At a vegetarian banquet in 1853, the gathered guests lifted their alcohol-free glasses to toast: "Total Abstinence, Women's Rights and Vegetarianism." In 1910, Canadian suffragists opened a vegetarian restaurant at their Toronto headquarters. *The Vegetarian Magazine* of the early twentieth century carried a column called "The Circle of Women's Enfranchisement."

Proponents of male dominance hedge no words in exclaiming

155

against vegetarianism because of a suspected anti-male bias. James Whorton quoted one response to a vegetarian regime of the 1830s which charged that "Emasculation is the first fruit of Grahamism." The Grimké sisters and Abby Kelley were among many abolitionists who adopted the Graham diet and truly did try to "emasculate" the patriarchal power enslaving African-American people.

Vegetarianism was an integral part of autonomous female identity. It was *de facto* a rebellion against the dominant culture. We learn from Mary Alden Hopkins, writing in the 1920s, that at one point in her life, she reacted "against all established institutions, like marriage, spanking, meat diet, prison, war, public schools and our form of government." Earlier, in 1852, Anne Denton, in "Rights of Women," published in *The American Vegetarian and Health Journal,* called upon women to develop their intellect, learn physiology, become vegetarians, and leave behind bourgeois patterns of behavior: "Women should live for something higher and nobler than cannibal tastes, good appearance, costly furniture or fine equipage." Mary Gove Nichols, nineteenth-century feminist and vegetarian, wrote of the new woman she anticipated: she "would not be the drudge of isolate household, cooking pork and other edibles for a gluttonous man." Instead, "she understands Water-Cure well; she is a good physician and a good nurse; she lives purely and simply on a vegetable diet; and is a water drinker." Nichols concludes: "Many such women are growing amongst us."

Many of these writers repeat a similar pattern which I call "the vegetarian quest," a three-part process including: an awakening in which the revelation of the nothingness of meat occurs, naming the relationship one sees with animals, and rebuking a meat-eating world.

The Nothingness of Meat

The first step in the vegetarian quest is experiencing *the revelation of the nothingness of meat as an item of food*, the realization that it came from something, or rather someone, who has been made into no-thing, no-body. The revelation can also be catalyzed when meat has been divested of any positive qualities with which it is usually associated. After the awakening to meat's nothingness, one sees that its sumptuousness derives from the disguises of sauces, gravies, marinades, and cooking, and that its protein is neither unique nor irreplaceable. In experiencing the nothingness of meat, one realizes that one is not eating food but dead bodies. Thus, George Sand stopped eating meat for two weeks after a grisly battle which left human corpses rotting within view of her window. Many report an epiphany that turns them away from meat, a moment of realization when they say, "What am I doing eating "meat?" Barbara Cook ascribes her *"awakening* to love" and animal rights activism to a time when she held a small calf in her arms, who "seemed the symbol of every new creature ever brought into the world." But she learned that this symbol often became veal, and thus the nothingness of meat was revealed to her: "For months afterward I cried when I thought of the calf. I cried when I saw milk-fed veal on a menu. The piece of pale flesh wrapped neatly in cellophane in the supermarket would never again be faceless masses."

Suffragist Agnes Ryan described becoming a vegetarian in a chapter called "I Meet a New Force" in her unpublished autobiography. When she began to prepare some meat, she realized that it was rotten. "The chops were spoiled. They had been frozen. The warmth of the room was thawing them out. I was horrified. It was a long time since I had known that smell. A terrible and devastating flood of thoughts began to pour in on me. Something true in my life was fighting for release." Memories, reactions, revulsion, reflections were triggered by the putrid meat: "Had I ever in my life been able to eat meat at all if I allowed myself to think of the living creature which had been deprived of life?"

Ryan reports that she had never heard of vegetarians, but "I thought of all the girls and women who loathed the handling of meat as I had done, and who saw no way out, believing that flesh food was necessary for bodily health and strength." Then she heard the president of the Millennium Guild, M. L. R. Freshel, speak out against meat eating, and her reaction was given a new context: "Here was a new type of woman, here was a new spiritual force at work in the universe. She clearly stressed the idea that wars will never be overcome until the belief that it is justifiable to take life, to kill—*when expedient*—is eradicated from human consciousness." According to Ryan's reconstruction of this event, the revelation of the nothingness of meat provided a context for reconsidering the role expectations for men and women in western culture. "I knew that men were not supposed to mind killing. Weren't men usually the butchers, the soldiers, the hangmen?" Through exposure to a female role model, M. L. R. Freshel, she found a context for interpreting the nothingness of meat in a warring world. Her revelation was undergirded by the connections between feminism, vegetarianism, and pacifism. In her eyes, this moment when she became a vegetarian was of such consequence that reflecting back on it she saw within it the origin for all the major positions she held for the next forty years.

Naming the Relationships

The second step in the vegetarian quest is *naming the relationships*. These relationships include: the connection between meat on the table and a living animal, between a sense that animals have rights and that killing them for meat violates those rights. The interpretation moves from the nothingness of meat to the statement that killing animals is wrong.

Identifying women's fate with that of animals appears in the naming stage as well: both are treated like pieces of meat in an androcentric culture, though in the case of women this is a metaphorical treatment. Women identify their own nothingness with that of animals when they talk of being treated like pieces of meat. In an epiphany in the life of Beth in the novel *Small Changes*, Marge Piercy links the double-edged nothingness. Beth, trapped in a marriage of domination and control, while eating meatloaf realizes that she is a "trapped animal eating a dead animal."

One aspect of naming is reclaiming appropriate words for meat, words which do not rely on euphemisms, distortions, misnaming. By reminding people that they are consuming dead animals, vegetarians point to the literal meaning of meat and refuse to allow the animal to be made absent. Elsa Lanchester describes how her mother, "Biddy" Lanchester, feminist, suffragette, socialist, pacifist, vegetarian, challenged the false labeling of meat. When Elsa refers to the word "offal," she explains, "Biddy the vegetarian inspired the use of this word: That's what meat was to her." By re-naming, vegetarians re-define meat and offer a vision of how human beings should see themselves in relationship to animals. Thus they favor the word "corpse" for dead animals—most often used when referring to humans—rather than the blander "carcass."

Naming the relationships requires defining meat eating. It is the epitome of the oppression of animals; it is to animals what white racism is to people of color, what anti-Semitism is to Jewish people, what homophobia is to gay men and lesbians, and what woman hating is to women. All lead to oppression by a culture which does not want to assimilate them fully on their grounds and with rights. Yet, an enormous void separates these forms of oppression of people from the form by which we oppress other animals. We do not consume people. We do consume the other animals. Meat eating is the most numerically extensive institutionalized violence against animals. It is also the most common form of contact between most people and animals. In addition, meat eating offers the grounds for subjugating animals: if we can kill, butcher, and consume them—in other words completely annihilate them—we may, as well, experiment on them, trap and hunt them, exploit them, and raise them in environments which imprison them, such as factory-food and fur-bearing animal farms.

Rebuking a Meat-Eating and Patriarchal World

Rebuking a meat-eating world is the final stage in the vegetarian quest. By its enaction, vegetarianism rebukes a meat-eating society because it proves that an alternative to meat eating exists and that it works. In the western world, vegetarians in great numbers are living free of heart attacks, bowel or breast cancer, or malnutrition—seeming to confirm the claims that humans are physiologically vegetarian. But many vegetarians do not rest with the proof of the healthfulness of the vegetarian body. They seek to change the meat-eating world. Vegetarian, pacifist, and feminist Charlotte Despard refused to allow meat to be served at a soup kitchen she sponsored during the Great War. Agnes Ryan planned a *Vegetarian Pocket Monthly*, a manual to provide interested readers with hints and thoughts on vegetarianism.

Since meat eating is associated with male power, vegetarianism does more than rebuke a *meat-eating* society; it rebukes a *patriarchal* society, giving a feminist meaning to the vegetarian quest. Henry Stevens—Agnes Ryan's husband—posits that humanity was initially vegetarian, goddess worshipping, and pacifist. A plant culture, which Stevens found to be anthropologically and horticulturally verified, was replaced by what he called a blood culture of meat eating and male dominance. Describing "The Rape of the Matriarchate" he writes, "The truth is that animal husbandry and war are institutions in which man has shown himself most proficient. He has been the butcher and the soldier; and when the Blood Culture took control of religion, the priestesses were shoved aside."

We cannot tell the truth about women's lives if we do not take seriously their dietary as well as other choices that are at odds with the dominant culture. Vegetarianism has historically spoken to women; they would not have adopted it, maintained it, proselytized for it, if vegetarianism were not a positive influence on their lives. This is a historical fact that must be accepted and then responded to by scholars studying women's lives and texts.

Because of its emphasis on the literal, vegetarianism experiences the same treatment as women's words. It is ignored. An analysis that trivializes or ignores the literal will distance itself both from women's words and words about dead animals. The result is an absorption of vegetarian women's activism and their writings into the literary and historical feminist canon without anyone's noticing what they are saying. The numerous individual feminists who became vegetarians—from the Grimké sisters to Frances Willard, Clara Barton, Annie Besant, Matilda Joslyn Gage, May Wright Sewall, and Mary Walker—evidence a pattern of challenging androcentric culture not only because it rendered women absent but also because it rendered animals absent. As women defined their own subjectivity, their autonomy, they released animals from the object category in which patriarchal culture had placed them.

Acknowledging the existence of the feminist-vegetarian quest helps place individual women's actions within a context that can make sense of their decisions. If I had not been a vegetarian, would Agnes Ryan's query to herself as it appeared in the manuscript listings of the Schlesinger Library on the History of Women in America—"Papers omitted in vegetarian novel, use in feminist novel?"—have prompted me to muse on how she could imagine transferring a section of a book with one theme to a book with another theme? Ryan's question revealed to me her feminist-vegetarian quest and a variation of it that I see posed to each of us: "Ethics used in enunciating feminist principles, use toward animals?"

Sources

Cook, Barbara. "The Awakening." *The Animal's Agenda*, November, 1985.

Hopkins, Mary Alden. "Why I Earn My Own Living." In *These Modern Women: Autobiographical Essays from the Twenties*, edited by Elaine Showalter. Old Westbury, NY: The Feminist Press, 1978.

Lanchester, Elsa. *Herself*. New York: St. Martin's Press, 1983.

Lorde, Audre. *Sister Outsider: Essays and Speeches*. Trumansburg, N.Y.: The Crossing Press, 1984.

Nichols, Thomas L., and Mary Gove Nichols. *Marriage: Its History, Character and Results: Its Sanctities and Its Profanities: Its Science and Its Facts*. New York: T. L. Nichols, 1854.

Piercy, Marge. *Small Changes*. Garden City, NJ: Doubleday, 1972.

Ryan, Agnes. "The Heart to Sing," unpublished autobiography, pp. 309 – 316. Material quoted from Agnes Ryan is found in the Agnes Ryan Collection at The Arthur and Elizabeth Schlesinger Library on the History of Women in America, Radcliffe College, Cambridge, Mass. Permission to use material provided by the Schlesinger Library and the late Henry Bailey Stevens.

Stevens, Henry Bailey. *The Recovery of Culture*. New York: Harper & Row, 1949.

Whorton, James C. "'Tempest in a Flesh-Pot': The Formulation of a Physiological Rationale for Vegetarianism." *Journal of the History of Medicine and Allied Sciences*, 32, No. 2 (April 1977).

A Woman Is a Horse Is a Dog Is a Rat:

An Interview with Ingrid Newkirk

Theresa Corrigan

Ingrid Newkirk is the National Director and co-founder of People for the Ethical Treatment of Animals (PETA), one of the largest animal rights organizations in the United States, with a membership of over 250,000.

Something has always drawn me to nonhuman beings. For example, when I was a little girl, I was taken to the Taj Mahal. While everyone was inside looking at the tombs and the jewels, the encrusted walls and so on, I was outside for six hours watching a chipmunk, completely absorbed. When finally I was dragged into the Taj, I was, quick as a wink, on the other side of it, bending over the back wall, watching the water buffalos and trying to figure out how to go down and pet them.

But my full animal consciousness was slow to develop. As a species we're all damnably slow to wake up to what we're doing to other animals. I look back, as most of us do I suppose, and try to figure out what led to my present way of thinking. I find, sadly, that I'm a wonderful specimen of compartmentalized thinking: that it took Thing A to get me to change one of my behaviors but that I had to wait for Thing B (which usually meant another animal or another person suffering and maybe a string of animals and people suffering) before I "got" the second realization.

For example, I was not raised vegetarian (which I regret very much). I didn't have the wherewithal to make connections, like Harriet Schleifer, who at the age of five saw her father pulling a fish out of the water and realized he was hurting a friend and stopped eating meat. When I was about six or seven, my family was staying in a chalet in France. I wandered around the corner after spending hours admiring some fluffy trousered chickens on the hillside and saw the cook with his axe on the chopping block. I stopped eating meat then ... I stopped *eating* at that point. As with most people today, I associated eating with eating meat, so if you didn't eat meat, you didn't eat. And that was my first vegetarian experience. But somehow I was persuaded by my mother to stop fasting and to start eating again. I still didn't eat chicken for a long time, but I ate lamb. Lamb became my favorite food, even though on the hillsides there were always lambs playing and sheep walking around with little bells on. But I hadn't had *that* experience so I was too stupid to cross the divide.

People who have an affinity to nonhuman beings are drawn like magnets to places where these individuals are suffering. It's a horrible thing—your car steering wheel turns to the right and off you go because down that lane there is a slaughterhouse or something. In India, where I spent most of my growing-up years, I saw incredible cruelties to animals. Once when I was fourteen, I was sitting in my dining room enjoying lunch when I saw an ox cart stop in front of the window. The ox was emaciated, weak and exhausted. He faltered under the heavy yoke of the cart, no longer able to move, despite the blows striking his back. As I watched, my heart in my mouth, the ox driver dismounted, raised the animal's tail, and thrust the driving stick—a heavy wooden pole—deep into the animal's rectum. The ox bellowed, stumbled, and collapsed. As I rushed out, screaming at the driver to stop, I promised myself that when I grew up I would come back to India to help animals escape such treatment.

My mother used to rescue buffaloes and bullocks who had collapsed, and rescue usually meant kill. We used to send them away to sleep forever. So I grew up with euthanasia being the biggest and best cure. We would take in stray dogs and cats and injured birds and so on. Now I look back on those times and think of all the foolish things I did: not knowing what squirrels ate or what sustained them, desperately loving them and not realizing that love was not enough—slowly and unknowingly killing them, mourning and going through all the religious rituals of their deaths which were absolutely, in retrospect, unimportant and stupid.

When I was older, I read a book which changed my life—*Animal Machines* by Ruth Harrison. I was on vacation and had decided to visit my parents who were staying in a very desolate part of Southern Ireland. I picked up this book in the library; it ruined the next many weeks. I spent my time crying in a hotel room, having had it just revealed to me how factory farms operated. I hadn't a clue until then; I had really thought that such abysmal cruelties somehow only took place in the East, not in so-called civilized countries. Now I find it offensive that Western people refer to the cruelties in Mexico or Africa or India as being worse than here when all they are is more obvious. In fact, here it's more insidious. Our society recognizes that cruelty to animals is something to be ashamed of, and so you can't have any of it in front of you on the street. All the cruelties are sanitized for us, and all the advertisers know it, the fur and the meat and the cosmetics industries know it, and so *no* nasty association is there for you to make unless you dig for it. But pain and suffering are often the hidden ingredients in each of these products. So we have to go behind the closed doors, behind the sanitized wrap and look at the truth.

But digging is not enough. We must get past the Nazi mentality. It's a pity there's not another word for it, but that's obviously what it is, isn't it? The tremendous ability to seal yourself off from the suffering of those who happen to be different. Of course, there couldn't be any beings more different than lizards and chickens and fishes. And even those beautiful cows—I passed two cows on a truck this morning; they had just angelic faces, not that it should matter. I can understand how difficult it is for people who have been brought up to think that spiders and snakes are ghastly and scary and ugly, but I don't understand how people can fail to see what they are doing to animals like seals or cows who have big eyes and lovely angelic faces and look at you imploringly.

We have the idea that we are *the* thinking animal, that instinct is somehow inferior to intellect, and that only we are intelligent. I mean, my god "we" can put a man on the moon—when actually most of us can't even fix a broken record player, let alone invent one. And maybe that's just understanding mechanics, not really thinking. The human brain doesn't seem to be that much better than other animals' brains. You see the chimpanzee mother behaving very much like the human mother and packs of male dogs behaving very much like packs of juvenile male humans. By and large we *don't* think; by and large, I think we've come to *believe* that we think. We've been conned into imagining that we're the most amazing creatures on the face of the earth with enormous cerebral cortexes who can absolutely understand anything when actually we just function. We get in the car and we go to work and we go to bed and we eat and excrete and do all the other things. Nor do I think we have a great deal of capacity for quickly understanding things. We have to suffer through things and use experience and gradually come to grips with something and *then* we have to fight our desire *not* to change as well as all that conditioning.

Like the chimpanzees, we have terribly aggressive streaks in us. A friend of mine has an interesting theory about how early human beings, as vegetarians, would spend the day gathering a nut here and a berry there and foraging for a leaf or a twig or a root and would spend the whole day, just as most other animals do, getting something to eat, and every little thing was low in calories, so you had to spend the whole day doing it. But now that everything's mechanized, you have all this surplus energy on your hands that you used to forage with and so you think, what the hell, I'll throw a rock instead of uprooting this plant. Or, I'll pave this patch of woods instead of rooting through it. I don't know if that's true, but I do know that our pomp and circumstance and our ceremony and a lot of our traditions are based on chest beating. We need to reevaluate those aggressions, rechannel or eliminate them, and perhaps go back to letting the fields and woods grow freely, then forage in them again.

While our aggressive streaks may be similar to chimps', our single most significant difference from other animals is our abuse of power, the amount of destruction we do. And nothing makes that clearer or more graphic than flying somewhere and looking down and seeing that there is virtually nothing left of the earth that isn't cultivated, built upon, manipulated in some way. It's frightening, the misuse of power. Flying over Nevada last night, the air was clear, and I could see vast expanses of land. There seemed to be very little encroachment and I thought, how wonderful. For a moment I thought, you dears, you're down there and you're okay; *we're* not there. Then I thought, oh wait a minute, Nevada and test sites, my god . . . it's there, it's just underground.

People frequently say that animals too are destructive, that they kill and eat each other, so why stop eating them? Ironically, one of the good things of our species is that we don't have to aggress to survive. We can survive on fruits and vegetables. Some people suggest that if we hunted respectfully and only killed what we consumed, that would be alright. I'm not of the school that says you can kill a deer, but if you say a few words over the deer, that somehow resolves your complicity or makes your action acceptable. I cannot believe that I would kill to survive, or that a few words would make it alright. I don't know why, other than my self-interest, that it's more important for me to live than for the deer to live. I could sit around and try to justify it and say that our species is going to be *the* species, perhaps—if we don't blow ourselves off the face of the earth—that can influence each other whereas a deer can't write a treatise. But deer have influenced people, like Ron Baker who wrote *The Great American Hunting Myth*. It was a deer who changed his mind, not another person. Other people made him hunt, if you will, and it was a deer who changed his mind. So I'm not sure that saying, well, as a human being you can talk to other human beings and change them more effectively than the deer even washes.

And then there's the issue of whether to support the killing of animals to feed other animals. I do know it's possible to convert small cats into vegetarians, into vegans. There is a vegecat supplement now with taurine in it, that you can feed together with tofu and other non-animal proteins. I also know that some people have taken snakes, who normally eat live food, and have successfully fed them canned dog food, which is largely filler, fiber with some meat in it. Often that question comes up in discussions of keeping exotic animals, like a lion, for example. But if someone lined up fourteen rabbits and one lion and said, "Alright here are fourteen of them for the next month, and here is one"—what difference does it make what package they're in? Would you kill the fourteen for the one?

We are enamored of so-called exotic animals. Exotica seduces us. It's alright to be titillated, I suppose, by something exotic. It's normal for someone to do a double take, if you see something that's out of the ordinary, and be thrilled by it. But if that results in us hurting those who are ordinary, that's wrong. It's like the Audubon Society, which has refused to help us with pigeons, saying that they're common. You have to have a bald eagle or a rare warbler. It's the same with the ordinary rabbits and chickens who die to keep the lion alive. These are very, very tough issues and thankfully most of us don't have to grapple with them. All most of us have to grapple with is the question of whether *I* should eat an animal today or not.

I remember a Charlton Heston film called "Soylent Green." I sat through it, amazed at the point the film was trying to make. Charlton Heston was absolutely hysterical and spent an hour and a half in the company of other people trying to stop the use of euthanized human beings (who had voluntarily given up, deciding that the world was too horrible to live in) as a food source for other human beings. The option would be, was, is to keep the slaughterhouses open and to take healthy nonhuman beings, who didn't want to go, kicking and screaming down the ramp. And I thought, how absurd that this man is running around, desperately trying to stop something which is much better than the alternative. Of course from a health perspective, eating humans wouldn't be better than eating nonhumans. We'd continue to have arteriosclerosis and cancer and all those things. I would say do the fruit and vegetable bit. Leave the bodies for the vultures, who have different digestive tracts than we do.

I eat no animals or animal products. I think the animal rights activist or the person who wishes to make a health point needs to try to set an example of eating habits. If you don't need it, and you know you don't need it, then don't use it, so you can show others it's not necessary. I have no problem from an ethical perspective in having symbiotic relationships, especially with res-cued animals. If you can truly help animals, and then they live out their lives with you as their protector from this horrible world, and if they happen to lay eggs or have other bits and pieces they don't need, then it's probably harmless to use them. My parents had some hens for awhile and years ago when I went to visit them, I would eat the eggs from those chickens. Then I thought, wait a minute—I need to set an example and not use any animal products so people will say, "Oh, you're not dead yet and you don't eat *any* of that stuff."

People often imagine it must be complicated to become a vegetarian. I think that reaction is born of fear of change. Once you change, it isn't complicated. And the more you change, the less complicated it is. You go to the store and if you have no restrictions on what you eat, there are five thousand things for you to decide: should you get Campbell's soup with bacon, should you get it with beef, should you get it with ham, or should you get another brand. There are many more decisions that you have to stop and think about. As you simplify your life and make your choices clearer, there are whole aisles you can miss in the grocery store. You don't even bother to go near them. And your shopping becomes faster and more efficient because you know what you're going to eat and what you're not going to eat. You could pick up a book like *The Joy of Cooking* and spend half an hour trying to decide which recipe you're going to choose unless you know that certain recipes are off-limits to you, then you simply look at the perhaps twelve available recipes and decide which one you're going to prepare and bomb off and get the ingredients.

The fear is of change. The problem, I think, is people resisting, imagining how hard it's going to be, rather than just doing it. It's not hard. And the longer you do anything, the easier it gets. In fact, your life becomes much much simpler. If you refuse to participate in animal suffering, there are still plenty of things you can eat and wear and be entertained by. Just because I have eliminated circuses and rodeo and abusive films and so on, that's not to say that I can't be entertained. An incredible number of things can entertain me, and it's the same in the grocery store. There is a wide variety of vegetarian cookbooks nowadays to choose from. So you can make your life as easy or your decisions as varied as you like. But there's no reason not to change. Just as you don't go to the fur rack—the first step really for most people who become aware of animal issues is to say, no more fur. And just as you would never walk into the fur store, you find yourself doing the same thing when it comes to down or leather or meat counters or eggs or cheese. They don't exist for you. The Kentucky Fried Chicken outlet does not exist for you. It's not a choice; it's not there.

I have a friend who's a retired librarian, who became a vegetarian for ethical reasons, perhaps forty years ago. She didn't know what to eat, so she would buy only vegetables and boil them or bake them. Today it's hard to imagine that anybody other than a tremendously spoiled person could cry deprivation. There are soy cheeses, soy ice creams, you can make mayonnaise and whipped cream and cheesecake out of soy. There are meat analogues made of wheat and gluten. Anything you have ever had a taste for that consisted of an animal product exists now in a substitute. And if you follow fashion, you can follow it as an animal person and be just as trendy, if not more so, than any non-animal person.

Not using animal products is easy. What is hard is being aware of the tremendous suffering of animals. Sometimes you say, I wish I'd never learned. In the movement, we have this joke about who ruined your life. Alex Pacheco and Peter Singer ruined my life. And sometimes people come up to me and say, "You're the one; you ruined my life. You told me thus and such that I didn't know before." At times you can't help but think to yourself, boy, I could have such fun if I didn't know. But more importantly, I wish everyone knew. If everyone knew then the burden wouldn't be so great because everybody, or most people, would be doing *something* and the whole situation would change.

Nowadays the hardest sights for me are happy animals. That may sound incredibly odd. But nothing can make me cry faster than happy animals, because I see and read about and watch and think about animals suffering every waking moment. But when I see an animal free or even a happy dog walking with somebody or a bird sitting somewhere getting a drink of water, it's so touching to me that it breaks my protective wall and that can just cause me to break down. I have to think of something else.

You do steel yourself. I learned this having been a humane officer and having to stand in people's yards or on people's farms and know that how I dealt with them and what I could persuade them to do was very important for the animal whose custody I was seeking. Perhaps the most valuable lesson I had to learn was that surrendering to one's own emotions helps no one. The sight of a dog who can barely stand, his ribs protruding like a coat rack, his tail tight beneath his legs, quaking in fear on his chain as he watches his abusive human approach, can make you want to cry or react violently. But a conscientious investigator must show no emotion because she knows that the animal depends on her professionalism to get him out of there permanently. We are in a country where the animal is no more than chattel, and the "owner's" rights always trump the dog's. The ability to persuade the person to give up that dog, to use the right degree of pressure, to do one's job without seeming personally involved, can mean everything, including life, to the animal. I had to play my cards right in order to save each animal. I think it was good training for my mental well-being, to be able to keep thinking of the goal and not to drown in the enormity of the problem.

Another device I use is to try *not* to look at the big picture. It's like the Augean stable, you get your teaspoon and you start digging it out and hopefully one day there will be an end to it. But if you look at the enormity of it, it can depress you to the point where you stop functioning. Someone told me a lovely story the other day about a child who was on a beach. He had found all the starfishes who had washed up, and he was carefully taking the starfish, one by one, and he would put them back in the tide and push them off. Some of them were washing up again on shore, and occasionally one would wash back out to sea and get going again. A fisherman came by and said, "Hey, what'cha doing?" The boy said, "Well, I'm taking these starfishes and putting them back in the water because they're stranded here." And the fisherman said, "Look how many there are. There are hundreds on this beach. You're never going to be able to save them all." To which the little boy replied, pointing, "Yes, but I can save this one and I can save this one and I can save that one . . ." And that's what I think we're doing. As you rarely see the tangible results of your work, you've just got to keep doing the little bit you can do and satisfy yourself with the fact that you're trying. Or you will go mad.

We all steel ourselves in different ways. I *cannot* watch the slaughter of an animal in a slaughterhouse anymore. I can't do it. I stop myself from going in anymore, because I believe that I would have to physically intervene—which might not be a bad thing to do, except it probably would accomplish almost nothing. I can look at footage from labs, but a slaughterhouse is off-limits for me mentally. We each do what we can; some of us are messengers, some of us are providers, some of us are conduits. I find people who are trying to resist basic changes ask about very complicated issues that they're not likely to have to deal with. They're like children posing impossible choice situations—you know, the what-ifs. When I was a child I had an odd fantasy: if someone kidnapped my mother and father and the only way they would release them is if I ate a live slug sandwich, would I do it? I used to pose this to myself, but without any thought about the slugs actually being involved players in the equation. (Now, of course, it's much more complicated because it isn't just my revulsion at eating such a sandwich, but the slugs' rights too.) A silly childhood game, but just like the what-ifs people use to resist acknowledging animal suffering. There's no harm in trying to follow your theories all the way to some kind of extreme, but there is harm if it distracts you from taking practical measures to change your inexcusable day-to-day exploitative behavior.

Someone once actually asked me, "What if you had to operate on fruit flies to save a child's life?" He prefaced this by saying, "Well, I can understand what you're saying about not buying cosmetics and toiletries and household products that are tested in rabbits' eyes or force-fed to rats and so on, *but* . . ." and, as I looked out at the audience, I knew that most of the people there had not made even those changes in their own bathrooms and kitchens. And here we were, seriously going to debate an issue that no one would ever have to encounter in their lives. I had to stop and think: understanding isn't enough—you have to change your habits.

Some people will go to great lengths to misunderstand what I am saying, like when I said, "a rat is a pig is a dog is a boy." This quote actually comes from an as-yet-unreleased animal rights record, and the exact lyric has a horse in it, whom I inadvertently omitted. This, of course, is the favorite quote used against me—to insinuate that I am a person who would kill your child to save a rat. Of course, that's not what it means. I don't think there is ever a situation in which you would have to decide whether to kill a child to save a rat or vice versa. It was used to point out that we all *feel*. And those examples are all mammals, which should make it even easier for people to understand. Just because you are closer to one or find one more attractive or more familiar doesn't mean that they don't all feel just as much.

The other quote that they love to use against me is: "Six million Jews died in World War II, but six billion chickens will die in slaughterhouses this year." But it was the interviewer—and of course it's always hostile interviewers who pose these things to you—who brought up Auschwitz. I said to him that *we* are the very people who would be fighting to get people out of the Auschwitzes because these are the modern Auschwitzes. It's not as if we are choosing who is most important—suffering is suffering, death is death, exploitation is exploitation, and violence is violence. Today's concentration camps happen to house six billion chickens. I mean, frankly, the bit about a rat is a pig is a dog is a boy, which our opposition chooses to interpret as a choice, was not meant to assume a choice. You shouldn't ever have to decide. Why poison the raccoon who gets into your garbage? It's simply a matter of inconvenience for you but life for the raccoon. People hate the rat out of a mythology, particularly the so-called laboratory rat, or Norwegian rat, who is not the ghetto rat, through no fault of either. But people decide that some life and death struggle exists between them and other animals, and there isn't. There should be an all-encompassing empathy, an all-encompassing protection—for humans and animals.

We set up a horrible hierarchy, believing that some humans are more important than others, that humans are more important than other animals. I recently talked to people in Texas who said that the Red Cross and government hurricane evacuation programs warned not to take pets with them to safety: humans should be saved, but animals shouldn't. And last night on ABC news they showed a black-and-white dog standing with a tag on; the commentator said, "These people got out too quickly and left their dog behind." I find that incredible.

In Hurricane Agnes, it was horrible. We were the only people on our little creek who didn't evacuate, even though the first floor of our house was completely underwater. We had nineteen cats and had decided that if we didn't have to move them, we wouldn't. We had bags and hampers and all sorts of containers, and a rowboat at the back door ready to go if necessary. It was only after the flood subsided that I found out that people had evacuated and left their rabbits to die in their hutches. The cold water had come up slowly and drowned them. They hadn't even opened the hutches. In a house just two doors down from us, as we went out in the rowboat looking for cats in trees (and we found those), we found a canary with pneumonia who had been abandoned in her cage.

I once picked up a dog who was starving by the roadside. It took us days and days to catch this dog. We traced her tag to find the person who had dumped her. After I established with the neighbors that the man we had located indeed had "owned" a dog who looked like this, I went to see him and got him to admit that he had dropped the dog off. I said, "How did you think the dog was going to survive?" And he said, "Oh, the weather's good and I imagine she could eat berries and roots and so on." And I said, "What did you tell your children?" And he said, "Oh, I told the children that I had found another home for her." And I said, "If you really believed that she would be okay in the woods and it was alright for her to eat berries, you would have been happy to share that information with your children." But in his heart of hearts, he knew he was wrong and he knew even his children would know he was wrong. So he had to concoct a lie.

As children most of us were probably lied to about animals. I used to win a duck at the fair every year when I came home from boarding school. I *never* thought about this for years: these were live ducks who swam around in a bathtub and you took a wooden hoop and tried to ring the duck, and every year I got one; it never occurred to me that there was anything wrong with bashing these ducks in the head with rings to win them. And every year I went off to school in spring and I would say to my mother, "You *will* look after Lucky, won't you?" And she would say, "Of course, I will." And of course, every fall when I would come home, there would be no Lucky. My mother would say, "Oh, Lucky was placed." There was no one to place Lucky with, so I'm sure Lucky was served with roasted potatoes at somebody's dinner table. People lie to children out of the best of intentions, to spare them something, because they don't recognize that there are other players in the equation—that the duck needs to be spared something too. But people assume the duck is not a player; it's just your child, you must protect your child from the ugly truth, instead of cleaning up the ugly truth.

When you think of animals as players, it changes your relationships with them. I try not to form attachments with animals, both for my sake and for theirs, although I must admit that my dog of seventeen and a half years, whom I euthanized two years ago, was the person I had spent more years with and was closer to than anyone in my entire life. Now I have a chihuahua mix who came to me by accident—I never thought of little dogs as my cup of tea, frankly, but this dog managed to wheedle her way into my heart. And I still have one old cat whom I share with a co-worker who has another lone cat, so these two cats have come to know each other, enjoying each other's company more than mine. I think that's healthier. I see it as a problem that so many animals are totally dependent on human beings; their lives revolve around the central human character, which is not good for them if something happens to you or you travel a lot or hold a full-time job or you end up in jail. Though I share my life with animals, I try to give them a life in which they have some interaction with other people and other animals so that my absence at any time is not going to be devastating to them—and I suppose I protect myself in the same way.

I also enjoy many other relationships with animals. One of our donors saved a pet cemetery, which is really a very special place, it turns out, that was about to be bulldozed. Office townhouses were to be put up on top of graves which go back to the 1920s. It's not a morbid place at all; the graves have pictures of animals and it's a wonderful tribute to how people's lives were shared with them. You can feel people's emotions in the inscriptions they chose for the stones. Although we intend to maintain the land for the ones who rest there, we also plan to use the grounds as a sanctuary for certain live animals who otherwise wouldn't have a place to go. We just bought five sheep from the 4H livestock auction, and we have turkeys who came off a truck that overturned en route to the slaughterhouse. We also have chickens who were rescued from the Santeria cult slaughter by a humane officer and so on. The happiest thing is, when I have to go up there to conduct business, I can spend time looking at them and admiring them and interacting with them.

When people ask me how I interact with the animals, as if I had a special way, I say I put a lampshade on my head and tell them a funny joke. But really I'm probably a pain in the neck to them because I'm always so much in awe of them all. (I think people would probably be much prettier if our faces were covered with fur and feathers.) It's probably pretty much a one-way relationship because these animals are so self-sufficient; they have their cliques and families and certainly don't need me to say hello to. It was different when I was a humane officer. In those situations they know that you're rescuing them, unless they're too far gone, unless they've had so many horrible experiences that they can no longer figure out what's going on. Animals know what you're about, and when you come to pull them out of the drainage ditch or take them off the chain or crawl under the house to get their maggot-infested bodies, they look at you and they assess that you are here to take them away. You're their angel. And they know, "Now I've been saved." There's reward and sadness in that. The bond is very deep, even if it lasts for a few hours and even if it ends with your sending them away, giving them the big sleep, which is the nicest thing humane officers can sometimes give animals.

The whole issue of euthanasia is a damned difficult one to resolve. I think, to be truly humane, you have to look at each individual circumstance in which you make the decision. I find it incredibly offensive that most people will give birth and bring a life into the world or think nothing of someone else bringing a life into the world, with all the complexity of that life, and on the other hand condemn any euthanasia or any taking of a life, no matter how crumpled and defeated and miserable that life is and how much it begs to go. A friend of mine who is a nurse worked in the intensive-care unit, and she would tell me that on the next floor it was all sunshine and light with babies being brought into the world and no one thinking twice about the complications, the responsibilities and so on of doing that. Whereas where she worked, there would be old people trying to pull the respirators out of their noses, trying to pull the intravenous hook-ups out of their arms, passing her notes saying,

"Let me die." And her job was to slot these things right back in and make sure that they stayed alive no matter how lousy their lives were. And what terrible mental anguish that she went through trying to juxtapose these two conflicting ideas.

Some people also deride those of us who support euthanasia, whether for people or for animals, by saying, well, you have no right to play god. But in a custodial relationship, if you opt not to euthanize, you are playing god just a surely as if you opt to euthanize. It has to do with guilt. You can apply this idea also to adoptions: re-homing of animals. Some people's criteria are very, very low, and they will pass an animal on without checking at all. They'll take the chance that that person is a research dealer or will keep the animal on a chain and not take the animal to a veterinarian or will allow the animal to reproduce—to clear their consciences of not having to kill that animal. Whereas from my perspective, I can sleep better at night knowing that that animal is permanently safe from all evil and harm since I have truly had the opportunity to see the extent of abuse, the volume of abuse, and the meager options. If there is an option better than death, fine. The question boils down to whether quality of life is a factor. I think the quality of a life is a big factor. If we were in Nazi Germany, which again seems to me to be the absolute analogy of so many of these situations, and a Nazi guard said to me, your mother's coming into this room and you can either have our guards punch and kick your mother and then put her in the gas chamber, or you can lead her in gently and make her sit down and be calm and so on, I would lead her in and try to make her last moments peaceful. Knowing that it is inevitable that she is going to suffer the other way, I would much rather sit her down. Now some people would find that absolutely appalling, but it's just practical; if you can give someone a few good minutes and then poof—they're gone without knowing it, without suffering, isn't that better than standing back and letting them suffer because you don't want to do a distasteful act? That's why I've spent a lot of my time working for euthanasia reform. Because it is going to happen until we can stop the "disposable animal" mentality of those who acquire, abuse, breed, and discard animals, we must make it happen painlessly while trying to re-duce the numbers and finally eliminating the numbers that have to be euthanized simply because they are a human waste disposal problem. The bottom line is that your personal guilt negotiations must not trump the interests of the subjects you're dealing with who depend on you to look after their interests first. Your psychological well-being must be secondary.

Much of all this killing results from people not spaying and neutering animals they live with. Some argue that sterilization is contrary to an animal rights perspective. Technically it is. Clearly it's a violation of a biological right, if you will. But it's a question of conflicting rights. We've domesticated dogs and cats, and so their reproductive systems are haywire, and they have many, many more offspring than they would if they were still wild and free. Twenty-some million have been discarded in pounds and shelters, and many more are discarded in other ways or live out miserable lives. Since we have caused an over-population problem, I think we have to deal with it. I don't think reproduction is as fundamental a right as the right to have a decent life. I'm an advocate of zero population growth for human beings, and I don't believe that I have missed anything by not having children. A mother might say, well, you don't know what you're missing because you've missed it. But I don't feel any suffering or loss at not having been a mother. And I imagine a cross section of the dog, cat, and deer population feel as I do.

Much of the oppression of women is related to motherhood. And the same is true of animals. Here I see a strong connection between feminism and animal rights, the most offensive, obvious one being the subjugation of their sexuality and the use of their reproductive ability for some exploiters' purposes—that chickens and cows and all the animals who bear offspring have had their reproductive capacities perverted for nothing more than some-body's taste buds. Control of your own sexuality and reproductive system is something every feminist understands for herself, yet so many women fail to extend their understanding of that prin-ciple to animal mothers. Predictably, it is the female animals who suffer the most on today's cruel, intensive factory farms. Their bodies are treated simply as meat, milk, and egg producing machines. Superovulated, artificially inseminated on a metal frame that farmers accurately call the "rape rack," cow mothers have their infants taken from them within a few hours or days of their birth. The calling of mothers and babies from their separate stalls is one of the saddest things I've ever heard. Their milk is stolen for human consumption. The calves raised for veal are chained inside small crates for the entire sixteen weeks of their lives. Laying hens live in concentration-camp conditions, five to seven of them in a space the size of a record album cover. They are under such stress from overcrowding and constant illumination that they frequently peck each other until they are bloody, featherless, and weak. They have absolutely no choice; they are totally enslaved. The plight of these animals reminds me of a chapter in Susan Griffin's book *Woman and Nature* in which she compares the descriptions of "breeder cows" with those of "breeder women" on the cotton plantations.

I think there are other connections between feminism and animal rights. I do subscribe somewhat to the theory of "woman as natural nurturer" in many situations. Most people in animal welfare are women. Women tend to be more comfortable showing sympathy and less embarrassed by their emotions. But the animal rights way of thinking doesn't necessarily involve nurturing—it's a commonsensical idea about our relationships with others. So you find the animal rights movement drawing more men. But again, the whole culture is, of course, evolving so that some men aren't so anxious to be macho. And of course the bad part of that is so many women are learning to be macho, which is utterly offensive. There are women going into experimentation and fishing and all sorts of other things. It's harder for me to see a photograph of a woman being abusive or to hear of a woman who performs really ghastly experiments. I'll always remember the picture of a woman at a dog fight. The two dogs are tearing each other apart and there's an all-male audience except for one woman who is cheering vigorously. It's much more offensive to me, as a woman, to see a woman doing that.

You know, my personal bias is that women are better at animals rights work than men, but I hope I'm wrong. I hope it's only a personal bias. I hope everybody is drifting in the same direction and that women have just got a head start.

Feminism deals with much more than the relations between the human genders. It deals with principles, and if we conveniently ignore the principles, we're reduced to a self-serving group. Feminists should uphold the rights of all those who are downtrodden, particularly those who cannot speak for themselves. It's the same with the peace movement—if you oppose war only as long as you or your loved ones are endangered by a particular war but forget about it when that war is over, you're not living up to your principles. They have got to be consistent. You've got to carry the principles across lines. If you're against violence, if you're against exploitation, if you're against oppression, then you *must* be for animal rights. Because any arguments against animal rights would mean that you're not really against those things.

A cow doesn't need the same rights as a person. She can't vote. But she can appreciate her life and her family. Yet the other animals' basic needs and simple pleasures are denied not out of human need but out of human greed.

The whole thrust of the animal liberation movement is to promote respect, sensitivity, and compassion. To change the "us or them" attitude that allows people to ignore, exploit and abuse others just because the "others" are somehow different. As Peter Singer said, "Difference never justified a moral prejudice." An animal rights philosophy helps us confront our prejudices, forbids us to perceive our encounters with nonhumans as power games, and reminds us that we have a responsibility not only to members of our own sex, our own family, our own race, our own species, but to all those who share the world with us.

I was recently looking at a book about elephants, *To Whom It May Concern* by David Gucwa, and found it quite disturbing. Perhaps the most disturbing part is the final picture in it, which is an elephant's eye, just the eye and the very, very wrinkled skin around the eye towards the bridge of the nose. If I hadn't known that that was an elephant's photograph, I would have thought it was a Tibetan woman, a peasant woman's eye. I know many of us have seen pictures of whales' eyes and thought, oh, my god, you know, there's somebody there. And this elephant's eye is the same. But the book is about art, the art of elephants, and a particular elephant who Gucwa, as a keeper, found drawing with a pebble on the ground. And so he gave her paper and crayons and she drew. Then he took her art to various experts and asked them to analyze it. And he found that she is well beyond the various stages of art that human infants go through before they're able to shove things into the center of the page and to grasp various concepts of how to portray things. So perhaps we're not even as different as we think.

Waking Up the Rake
Linda Hogan

In the still dark mornings, my grandmother would rise up from her bed and put wood in the stove. When the fire began to burn, she would sit in front of its warmth and let down her hair. It had never been cut and it knotted down in two long braids. When I was fortunate enough to be there, in those red Oklahoma mornings, I would wake up with her, stand behind her chair, and pull the brush through the long strands of her hair. It cascaded down her back, down over the chair, and touched the floor.

We were the old and the new, bound together in front of the snapping fire, woven like a lifetime's tangled growth of hair. I saw my future in her body and face, and her past was alive in me. We were morning people, and in all of earth's mornings the new intertwines with the old. Even new, a day itself is ancient, old with earth's habit of turning over and over again.

Years later, I was sick, and I went to a traditional healer. The healer was dark and thin and radiant. The first night I was there, she also lit a fire. We sat before it, smelling the juniper smoke. She asked me to tell her everything, my life spoken in words, a case history of living, with its dreams and losses, the scars and wounds we all bear from being in the world. She smoked me with cedar smoke, wrapped a sheet around me, and put me to bed, gently, like a mother caring for her child.

The next morning she nudged me awake and took me outside to pray. We faced east where the sun was beginning its journey on our side of earth.

The following morning in red dawn, we went outside and prayed. The sun was a full orange eye rising up in the air. The morning after that we did the same, and on Sunday we did likewise.

The next time I visited her it was a year later, and again we went through the same prayers, standing outside facing the early sun. On the last morning I was there, she left for her job in town. Before leaving, she said, "Our work is our altar."

Those words have remained with me.

Now I am a disciple of birds. The birds that I mean are eagles, owls, and hawks. I clean cages at the Birds of Prey Rehabilitation Foundation. It is the work I wanted to do, in order to spend time inside the gentle presence of the birds.

There is a Sufi saying that goes something like this: "Yes, worship God, go to church, sing praises, but first tie your camel to the post." This cleaning is the work of tying the camel to a post.

I pick up the carcasses and skin of rats, mice, and of rabbits. Some of them have been turned inside out by the sharp-beaked eaters, so that the leathery flesh becomes a delicately veined coat for the inner fur. It is a boneyard. I rake the smooth fragments of bones. Sometimes there is a leg or shank of deer to be picked up.

In this boneyard, the still-red vertebrae lie on the ground beside an open rib cage. The remains of a rabbit, a small intestinal casing, holds excrement like beads in a necklace. And there are the clean, oval pellets the birds spit out, filled with fur, bone fragments, and now and then, a delicate sharp claw that looks as if it were woven inside. A feather, light and soft, floats down a current of air, and it is also picked up.

Over time, the narrow human perspective from which we view things expands. A deer carcass begins to look beautiful and rich in its torn redness, the muscle and bone exposed in the shape life took on for a while as it walked through meadows and drank at creeks.

And the bone fragments have their own stark beauty, the clean white jaw bones with ivory teeth small as the head of a pin still in them. I think of medieval physicians trying to learn about our private, hidden bodies by cutting open the stolen dead and finding the splendor inside, the grace of every red organ, and the smooth, gleaming bone.

This work is an apprenticeship, and the birds are the teachers. Sweet-eyed barn owls, such taskmasters, asking us to be still and slow and to move in time with their rhythms, not our own. The short-eared owls with their startling yellow eyes require the full presence of a human. The marsh hawks, behind their branches, watch our every move.

There is a silence needed here before a person enters the bordered world the birds inhabit, so we stop and compose ourselves before entering their doors, and we listen to the musical calls of the eagles, the sound of wings in air, the way their sharp-clawed feet, many larger than our own hands, grab hold of a perch. Then we know they are ready for us to enter.

The most difficult task the birds demand is that we learn to be equal to them, to feel our way into an intelligence that is different from our own. A friend, awed at the thought of working with eagles, said, "Imagine knowing an eagle." I answered her honestly, "It isn't so much that we know the eagles. It's that they know us."

And they know that we are apart from them, that as humans we have somehow fallen from our animal grace, and because of that we maintain a distance from them, though it is not always a distance of heart. The places we inhabit, even sharing a common earth, must remain distinct and separate. It was our presence that brought most of them here in the first place, nearly all of them injured in a clash with the human world. They have been shot, or hit by cars, trapped in leg hold traps, poisoned, ensnared in wire fences. To ensure their survival, they must remember us as the enemies that we are. We are the embodiment of a paradox; we are the wounders and we are the healers.

There are human lessons to be learned here, in the work. Fritjof Capra wrote: "Doing work that has to be done over and over again helps us recognize the natural cycles of growth and decay, of birth and death, and thus become aware of the dynamic order of the universe." And it is true, in whatever we do, the brushing of hair, the cleaning of cages, we begin to see the larger order of things. In this place, there is a constant coming to terms with both the sacred place life occupies, and with death. Like one of those early physicians who discovered the strange inner secrets of our human bodies, I'm filled with awe at the very presence of life, not just the birds, but a horse contained in its living fur, a dog alive and running. What a marvel it is, the fine shape life takes in all of us. It is equally marvelous that life is quickly turned back to the earth-colored ants and the soft white maggots that are time's best and closest companions. To sit with the eagles and their flute-like songs, listening to the longer flute of wind sweep through the lush grasslands, is to begin to know the natural laws that exist apart from our own written ones.

One of those laws, that we carry deep inside us, is intuition. It is lodged in a place even the grave-robbing doctors could not discover. It's a blood-written code that directs us through life. The founder of this healing center, Sigrid Ueblacker, depends on this inner knowing. She watches, listens, and feels her way to an understanding of each eagle and owl. This vision, as I call it, directs her own daily work at healing the injured birds and returning them to the wild.

"Sweep the snow away," she tells me. "The Swainson's hawks should be in Argentina this time of year and should not have to stand in the snow."

I sweep.

And that is in the winter when the hands ache from the cold, and the water freezes solid and has to be broken out for the birds, fresh buckets carried over icy earth from the well. In summer, it's another story. After only a few hours the food begins to move again, as if resurrected to life. A rabbit shifts a bit. A mouse turns. You could say that they have been resurrected, only with a life other than the one that left them. The moving skin swarms with flies and their offspring, ants, and a few wasps, busy at their own daily labor.

Even aside from the expected rewards for this work, such as seeing an eagle healed and winging across the sky it fell from, there are others. An occasional snake, beautiful and sleek, finds its way into the cage one day, eats a mouse and is too fat to leave, so we watch its long muscular life stretched out in the tall grass. Or, another summer day, taking branches from flight cages to be burned near the little creek, we see a large turtle with a dark and shining shell slipping soundlessly into the water, its presence a reminder of all the lives beyond these that occupy us.

One green morning, an orphaned owl perches nervously above me while I clean. Its downy fathers are roughed out. It appears to be twice its size as it clacks its beak at me, warning me: stay back. Then, fearing me the way we want it to, it bolts off the perch and flies, landing by accident on the wooden end of my rake, before it sees that a human is an extension of the tool, and it flies again to a safer place, while I return to raking.

The word "rake" means to gather or heap up, to smooth the broken ground. And that's what this work is, all of it, the smoothing over of broken ground, the healing of the severed trust we humans hold with earth. We gather it back together again with great care, take the broken pieces and fragments and return them to the sky. It is work at the borderland between species, at the boundary between injury and healing.

There is an art to raking, a very fine art, one with rhythm in it, and life. On the days I do it well, the rake wakes up. Wood that came from dark dense forests seems to return to life. The water that rose up through the rings of that wood, the minerals of earth mined upward by the burrowing tree roots, all come alive. My own fragile hand touches the wood, a hand full of my own life, including that which rose each morning early to watch the sun return from the other side of the planet. Over time, these hands will smooth the rake's wooden handle down to a sheen.

Raking. It is a labor round and complete, smooth and new as an egg, and the rounding seasons of the world revolving in time and space. All things, even our own heartbeats and sweat, are in it, part of it. And that work, that watching the turning over of life, becomes a road into what is essential. Work is the country of hands, and they want to live there in the dailiness of it, the repetition that is time's language of prayer, a common tongue. Everything is there, in that language, in the humblest of labor. The rake wakes up and the healing is in it. The shadows of leaves that once fell beneath the tree the handle came from are in that labor, and the rabbits that passed this way, on the altar of our work. And when the rake wakes up, all earth's gods are reborn and they dance and sing in the dusty air around us.

Sweet William
Theresa Corrigan

"Death has no power over the feeling of Sweet William's breath on my fingers." —Pat Derby, who saved William from being executed.

Black bear
over the hill nose
scarred pads
rag tag rump,
you are my totem.

Sing to me the howl of resistance.
Dream to me the forests of your heart.

Like the dragon
slain to make men
larger than life,
you met your saint george—
in the circus.
Armed with whip and chains,
he fought to claim your spirit,
four times broke your nose.
Like Stepin' Fetchit
you danced the Fool
on fire scarred pads
till rage burned murder into your eyes.

Now your cloudy eyes
mirror prisms of lost souls,
death marches,
slaveships,
burnt offerings

to ancient gods.
Your deep throaty rumblings
call up the keening
of war land mothers.

Descendant of your primordial enemy
I would expect vengeance from you.
Instead you make my heart soar
with your gentle nudging.

Sweet William,
I too can be of stout heart
and steady gaze
when enemies threaten to plant
seeds of bitterness in my soul.
I too can keep dreams of wildness
alive in my spirit
when those who would chain me
capture my devotion.
I too can claim my animal forgiveness
when fury devours my soft underbelly.
I must only remember the first time
you kissed me,
sliding your smooth ragged tongue
along the side my face.

William, sing to me the howl of resistance.
Dream to me the forests of your heart.

IV.

In our selves and lives
it has surely only begun.

Paper into Flesh into . . .
Stephanie T. Hoppe and
Theresa Corrigan

Over the now several years of our searching, collecting, negotiating, thinking, and rethinking *With a Fly's Eye, Whale's Wit, and Woman's Heart* and *And a Deer's Ear, Eagle's Song, and Bear's Grace*, the two volumes of the anthology have also been disassembling, editing, and reassembling us. That process is what we wish to account for here.

It began with our meeting at a week-long women writers' workshop in Oregon—most particularly, with the evening readings in which the poems and stories that the different women had written alone and apart were brought together with a complex interweaving of common experiences and individual voices and perspectives that added up to far more than the sum of the parts. The idea we had was to bring this multiplicitous, enriched perspective to bear upon a single subject, a subject that was particularly important to the two of us: our dealings as human women with the other animals who inhabit this world.

From the start we knew we wanted writings not just by women or about animals but fully involving both; writings that explored the relationships between beings of different species, describing things as they are and searching for things as they might better be. We found, as in fact we had hoped, more than we ever dreamt of—a community of women that extends around the world, women linked to each other by many years of working and thinking about these issues, and each representing the community of diverse species in which she lives. We found writers like Sally Carrighar, Sally Miller Gearhart, Judy Grahn, and Ursula K. LeGuin, who work at shaping the languages we need in order to more clearly perceive and talk and think about these things that concern us, and others like Chrystos, Linda Hogan, and Mary TallMountain, who remind us of older ethics that recognize the kinship of geography and animals, including humans. We found women like Hope Sawyer Buyukmihci, who founded a wildlife refuge in New Jersey where she has also lived for thirty years and raised her own family; women like Ingrid Newkirk, an activist who both rescues individuals and works to end all abuse; and Carol J. Adams and Sally Roesch Wagner, scholars who contribute to the political and historical context we need in order to appreciate the implications and possibilities of our individual experience.

I

Western thought has long and unquestioningly linked women and other animals. But what, precisely, are these links? What, for that matter, are "animals"? We humans call ourselves animals, at least sometimes, in some senses of the word. At other times, we distinguish animals from ourselves as well as from birds, insects, fish, and other beings. Many human languages lack any term for the full range of living beings, let alone the range we had in mind, of all conceivable beings, including the imaginary and otherworldly.

The words the English language affords for animals—beast, brute, creature—are often as pejorative as its terms for women (and denigrated classes of men). I Theresa begin my "Introduction to the Women's Movement" course by asking the students to make a list of terms that apply to women; a majority are always animal names that further the stereotypes of women and of other animals. "She's a real dog." "A hen-pecked husband." A young woman may be referred to as a "chick"—fluffy, vulnerable, soft—but when she ages she becomes a "hen," who is presumed to be a stupid, squawking egg layer. In scorn, hate, and fear, as well as sometimes with affection (if condescending), women are called foxes, kittens, sows, cows, nags, fillies, tuna, vixens, and on and on. Terms for relationships continue the pattern: "the wife," "the family pet," "livestock" are institutions, objects of possession, not individual beings. Women and other animals may be not so much identified with each other as jointly objectified and excluded from Western cultural perspectives. As Susan Griffin writes in *Woman and Nature:*

He says that woman speaks with nature. That she hears voices from under the earth. That wind blows in her ears and trees whisper to her. . . But for him this dialogue is over. He says he is not part of this world, that he was set on this world as a stranger. He sets himself apart from woman and nature.

Animals are indeed common subjects in women's writing and art . . . but in what ways? To what ends? As with so many other forms of expressive behavior deemed trivial in themselves and permissible to women but not to men, it is "all right" for women to be fond of animals, especially "cute" ones—but if we step beyond private attachments to politically champion animal rights or intellectually analyze our parallel oppression, that is another matter! The field study of living animals, a branch of science where women can be found in some numbers, is itself often considered only marginally scientific. Thus, questions gathered around us like spectral beings. . . .

We had thought fiction and poetry would lead the way, modeling dreams, challenging assumptions and conventions, opening new vistas, but as we began to review manuscripts, we instead learned anew the power of fiction and poetry to embody and perpetuate fixed and inflexible ways of thinking. Through long gray winter weeks we received poems, stories, reminiscences of dead animals. Disease. Euthanasia. Accidents. Neglect. Roadkills. Days passed in which we thought the only remaining interactions that U.S. women have with members of other species occur on the other side of their automobiles. Or mediated by the veterinarians who euthanize animals that are hurt, sick, frightened, aging, surplus, or simply gone out of fashion. The lives of animals seemed to be told only as context for their deaths, with a frightening repetitiveness of stock events (the cuteness of infancy, the mischievousness of youth, a near loss prefiguring the final separation). Even the deaths were rarely acknowledged as being the *animals'*. The mercy killing of an injured deer or the last illness of an aged companion cat was documented as a vicarious experience of the woman who observed it or as a teaching tool for her children; an occasion for her philosophical speculations on the nature of mortality or an opportunity to express her grief over one or many human deaths for which the animal stood in as symbol. We reminded each other of Edgar Allen Poe proclaiming a century ago that the highest and most affecting subject, the most proper topic for literature, was the death of a beautiful woman. Were we seeing the same old story with only a change of personnel?

Many writings by women and most by men simply equated women with animals, dissolving the dignity of individual being in a symbolic identification with the (generally lost) natural world. Or they demanded that animals serve as teachers, inspirers, saviors; endlessly, patiently bearing the intrusion of human attention.

Nor did we find that a consciously feminist perspective necessarily ensured the questioning of cultural assumptions about animals. Many feminists seem to view their private lives with other animals as unconnected to everyday political realities—indeed a respite from politics, a topic apart where one may lay aside the struggle for consciousness. We discovered that much recent fiction by women about animals follows a pattern: a situation of extreme patriarchal domination from which a woman, often timidly and always briefly, ventures into that traditionally blurred area between Woman and Nature, a setting similar to a dream or fantasy sequence that is carefully distinguished from the larger reality. While she may deal sensitively with animals she encounters, she makes little effort to integrate her experience into the rest of her life or the "larger," "real" world to which she grants primacy. The animals usually die.

Other feminist analysis uses atrocities done to animals to further, by comparison or metaphor, investigations of the exploitation of women: women are shown as further subordinated because of their actual, or perceived, link with nature, not-human, animal. Feminists who consciously or unconsciously embrace biological determinism often extol Woman's "natural" ties to Nature as indicative of her superior capacity for nurturance. All of these perspectives deny animals existence as inhabitants of their own realities; whether the comparisons illustrate or romanticize, they exploit animals for the human-centered purpose of discussing ourselves.

Remembering the insightful explorations of many science fiction/fantasy novels of the 1960s and 1970s, we looked forward to submissions of genre stories, but the stories we received more often portrayed imaginary beings as either cute and cuddly and quickly reduced to pet status or (like those giants of the silver screen, King Kong, Godzilla, Mothra) as ugly and deadly and "needing" to be exterminated; aliens were either clearly inferior animals or fully, if sometimes nastily, human. The preoccupation with maintaining species distinctions (with a rigor reminiscent of Ku Klux Klan views on racial purity) perhaps reflects the shift in U.S. society as a whole in recent years toward repression and rigidity. As more than one writer has pointed out, the question seems inconceivable—to humans—of beings arriving on Earth such that we can't tell whether they are whales, say, or people.

We turned, with a new suspiciousness, to nonfiction. What, we wondered, is the significance of the great popularity with large mainstream publishers and, apparently the public, of wildlife studies like those by Jane Goodall, Dian Fossey, Shirley Strum, Cynthia Moss, Hope Ryden, which we also eagerly devoured? How much of the experience of either the women or the animals they lived with and studied survives the editorial and marketing process that we already know strongly censors the perceptions and the behavior of women? Is there an undertext we might do well to heed: a story of gorillas, wild horses, orangutans, and others so near extinction as to be no longer competitive or threatening to the partriarchal order; a story of women, in devoting themselves to something like a deathwatch over species, displaying appropriately feminine compassion?

We believe these women are both brave and admirable, but we wonder how their surely varied individual experiences can turn out so much of a pattern. Dian Fossey's *Gorillas in the Mist* is an example: clear, engaging, and engaged-seeming writing— but by her own testimony she was only impatient with the writing of the book, doing it as quickly as she could to raise money for the gorillas. How much have we lost, irretrievably since her murder, that she alone perceived, but lacked time, interest, or editorial freedom to tell us?

We looked closer to home at women we know who work with animals in our own communities. Stephanie interviewed Jean Bilyeu (in *With a Fly's Eye*) about her day-to-day work like housekeeping, picking up after the messes made of animals' lives in Ukiah, California. Theresa interviewed Pat Derby (also in *With a Fly's Eye*), founder of the Performing Animal Welfare Society (PAWS) and a refuge for exotic animals, a woman one is as likely to encounter in jeans shoveling elephant dung as elegantly dressed—and eloquent—in the corridors and committee rooms of the state legislature. Theresa flew to Oregon one weekend for the interview with Ingrid Newkirk, founder of People for the Ethical Treatment of Animals (PETA), that is included in this volume. (Ingrid first told Theresa the standing joke in the animal activist community that the one who raises your consciousness to the point where you can no longer bear the contradictions you have lived with and must deal with them is the one who "ruined your life"; Ingrid ruined Theresa's.)

From the outset we wanted diversity, in species of beings as well as genres and perspectives of writings, but the largest number of submissions, which the finished volumes also represent disproportionately, concerned domesticated dogs and cats. These are the animals lived with most intimately, over long periods of time, by women who write, and we wanted precisely the results of close observation and long pondering. It struck us also that life with domesticated animals is no trivial subject— rather, it has been intertwined with human sociability and domesticity from perhaps earliest times.

The raising by humans of infant animals, whether stolen from their homes or orphaned by chance or hunters, may be as old as human culture. Since the core of human society is the willingness to care for young not one's own—a sister's or companions' offspring—the transference of caring seems likely to have been extended to the young of other species. Women can still be seen suckling orphan puppies and lambs, and surely we always did. No society seems ever to have made a new discovery immediately central to its survival. As in historic times iron was first used for jewelry and toys and only later for tools and weapons, it is likely animals were first domesticated for love or pleasure or play and only subsequently put to economic uses. We may yet find through domestication a means to fuller and joint socialization of humans and other animals.

I Stephanie believe house cats, for good and ill, are as irretrievably committed to civilization as women are. The cat who lives with me, Vanessa, chooses—and she does have alternatives—to spend most of the hours I work on the windowsill above my desk. Much of the time she sleeps, but she often also seems to keep watch, indoors and out, for things I don't myself consciously perceive: mischievous elementals, the forces that Luisah Teish advises periodically cleansing a house of, mini-black holes, shadow masses. . . . I am willing to believe that Vanessa's watch (in ways and for purposes she chooses and values) maintains our shared household and forwards work that often seems to me more than mine alone.

It is supposedly in the nature of small cats to live solitarily, but they obviously share the considerable capacity for social interaction that all mammals (and probably most other beings) possess. As I observe the visibly complex and shifting interactions between Vanessa and other cats in our neighborhood (and some dogs), I think I can pick out components of human as well as cat sociability. And as they have learned from us, so I also see the humans in this household change with increasing acquaintance of different cats. More and more, I question species distinctions, originating as they do in the reductive and rationalizing mind-set of eighteenth-century European thought, based ultimately on the single narrow point of reproductive fertility; distinctions that seem to me, like physiological distinctions of gender, likely to distort or obscure far more meaningful differences within groups as well as similarities across the lines.

I Theresa have always lived in close association (as Sally Carrighar puts it) with *many* animals, in response to what I believe to be their desires as well as mine. I want, quite simply, to provide a safe home to as many animals as I can responsibly handle and to develop bonds of trust and friendship with them. They, I think, benefit from being close to their species kin. Though I admit to fantasies of being the sole human in an animals' world, particularly when my shame at human atrocities becomes overwhelming, in reality I know I would miss something, communication of a sort particular to my species, reflections on which to pattern my behaviors, confirmation of me as human. I believe other animals deserve the same.

Living one's life without same-species contact is a situation few animals face unless they are domesticated or captive. Behaviors specific to each species, such as grooming, hunting or foraging techniques, play activities, I think are difficult to learn without models. Kittens separated from their mothers too young often lack skill at personal grooming. Mica, a wolf at the PAWS refuge, is nervous and timid, as a result (according to Pat Derby) of living without a pack.

Ted, a dog I have lived with for many years, spent several months of her puppyhood in the sole company of me and four-teen cats. She learned to lick her hand to wash her face, to stretch out long in the sun, and to use the litterbox (none of which were taught by me). She never barked. Then we went camping one weekend, and she met her first dogs. She seemed both excited and perplexed, running at them but not sniffing or sidling up in the usual dog hello way. When the first one barked at her, she ran to me. By the end of the weekend, she ran with the pack, still checking in with me periodically, but she seemed to see herself as dog and love it.

Of course, this account relies entirely on my observation and interpretation, but it reinforced in me the belief that we all benefit from seeing ourselves reflected back by other members of our particular species. I do not mean to imply that we must strictly adhere to only our own species traits; if anything, humans would do well to relax the boundaries we so carefully construct between ourselves and other species. But I do feel that we need to carefully consider the environments we create for those who share them with us. Ted was enriched by her cat models and learned much about survival in a human-constructed environment from me, but her dog self responded very specifically to her dog contacts.

It seems clear that dependency thwarts growth. The material circumstances of modern U.S. houses, and dangers such as au-tomobile traffic, necessitate a certain physical dependency: domestic animals must wait for food to be placed out, doors opened, litterboxes cleaned. The very number of animals who share my home at present (eleven cats and two dogs) does reduce their emotional or psychic dependency on me. They are able to meet many of their affectional needs with each other; they play, groom, spat, and sleep with each other, as well as at times with me. If one of them wants me and I'm busy, I notice he or she will seek out another member of the family. Sometimes if I attempt to join in their play, they will take their game to another room. I am not the center of their universes, anymore than any one of them is the center of mine.

In the Western world, with urbanization and suburbanization, fewer and fewer people have any intimate contact with non-domesticated animals. We anthropomorphize those outside our immediate reality: turn bears into Teddys, mice into Mickeys, elephants into Dumbos. In the absence of the real referent, the stereotypes embedded in these characters shape our understanding and capture our allegiance. The actual animals become nasty creatures to be hunted, trapped, or utilized as ornaments on our bodies or the walls of our houses while we sentimentalize the caricatures. One could argue that such anthropomorphizing leads to greater identification and thus greater affection; after all, what harm came come from loving one's teddy bear? Recently, in a toy store, I Theresa noticed a large number of stuffed animals made with skins of real animals. I was struck by the irony of humans destroying living beings only to reconstruct them and attach greater affection to their own creations. It would seem that many humans are unable to tolerate that which they cannot contain. "Pets" are contained in a network of dependency and training, "exotics" in zoos and circuses, the so-called useful animals in laboratory cages and factory farms, all others in man-made and marketable images and packaging.

When it comes to the sexuality of animals, U.S. literature seems even more than ordinarily prudish. As Mary Allen points out in *Animals in American Literature*, the animals of fiction—which are disproportionately male—are seldom shown as mates or fathers; much like human males in the same literature they generally lack social context of their own or other species. Women as well as men writers, who have begun to accept female humans as legitimate characters, have yet to extend their practice to other species: fiction continues routinely to assume male gender in animal characters not visibly mothering.

Like sexual encounters between human adults and children, in practice interspecies sexuality can hardly be anything other than abusive, taking place at the human adult's option and under conditions in which the animal, like the child, is unlikely to be able to effectively say yes or no. We found a charming exception in Alix Kates Shulman's "A Story of a Girl and Her Dog" (in this volume), which depicts the sexual awakening and play of a pair of younglings from two different species. Another fascinating examination into the topic is *Bear*, a novel by Marian Engel that graphically portrays a highly erotic relationship between a woman and a bear. *Bear* illustrates the sensitivity of the subject to context: we had some thought of seeking permission to reprint an excerpt, but found that without the context of the entire development of the novel and the particularity of the relationship, individual segments took on a false air of exploitive sensationalism.

Domestic dogs and cats are generally portrayed in fiction as surgically neutered, but in *Particularly Cats*, Doris Lessing describes a very different life with cats before the advent of the cheap and safe spay, and she wonders whether tubal ligations for female cats might allow them an active sex life free of the burden (to both cat and humans) of kittens. One of our veterinarians doubted the feasibility: lacking the hormones produced by pregnancy, a cat would come into heat and permanently remain in that state. She would have sex and nothing but sex. The veterinarian added that spayed and neutered cats live longer.

The cats I Stephanie have known who have borne kittens seemed to take no great pleasure in the process, appearing as harried as other mothers of my acquaintance. Both Theresa and I are childless by choice, and we may lack interest or sympathy. But we question the argument that spaying cats is unpardonably intruding on the fullness of their lives. Obviously it is a significant bodily interference; but so is killing and unwanted millions of offspring of cats and dogs and others who end up in shelters and pounds every year in the United States. In any species, our sensual, even our sexual, natures are hardly limited to genital experience.

I Theresa have found tremendous variation in the mothering capabilities and interests of animals with whom I have lived. Those who seem particularly interested in parenting adopt (a solution I wish more humans would consider). My friend Ted, a spayed maltese-poodle, loves babies of any sort, kittens will do, ducklings are fine. People would say, "Poor Ted, she should have been a mother!" But mothering, as many feminists recognize, is more than physically birthing. Spaying Ted did not deprive her of the maternal experience.

Nor are animals in the wild routinely or uniformly reproductive. Sally Carrighar noted in *The Twilight Seas* that an estimated forty percent of passerine birds never mate, and one can easily see the benefits to a species of a proportion of adults remaining unburdened by young in order to explore more fully both their capacities and their environment and to establish and maintain a reserve of knowledge and flexibility in case of circumstances changing. Pamela Uschuk's poem "Cultivating Stony Ground" (in this volume) illustrates important aspects of the operation of this principle in women's lives.

George Schaller, who has devoted much of his life to observing animals, writes that he believes that virtually all animals, if they lived in a situation where they could look beyond the most immediate urgencies of life and death would develop personalities such that humans would readily acknowledge.

To this, Theresa responds: animals already have fully distinct personalities—if only we look with eyes that can see. Studying wild horses in Nevada, Hope Ryden reached a similar conclusion, as she reports in *Mustangs:*

> Though I looked for sameness (the inductive method by its very nature calls for the enumeration of an unlimited number of similar histories), I soon realized that I was actually more interested in the individuality of the animals I watched. In fact, I began to comprehend the magnitude of the role of idiosyncratic behavior in the scheme of things. Diversity is actually the creative element in the evolutionary process; whereas, the conformity we like to measure is merely the "setting" of nature's wild impulses after these have proved successful over long ages of natural selection.

As too often when viewing other humans, we stereotype animals' behavior. We allow ourselves to think we know more about them than we actually do, and so let ourselves off from making closer observation: cats are aloof, chimps are so humanlike, baboons are happy when they smile. Or we separate ourselves from those we observe and ascribe threatening motives to their behavior: pit bulls are mean, elephants "need" to be dominated.

I Stephanie often think of the care taken by the human characters in Shirley Graves Cochrane's story "Rescue" (in *With a Fly's
Eye*) to address the animals courteously. And of Pat Derby's concern about caging the rescued exotic animals in her care—the
attention she pays to minimizing their frustration over their loss
of choices; being careful, for example, to notice whether they
wish one to approach or depart. I think of Vanessa's obsession
with doors; she goes through every door we open, often apparently without thinking about it and immediately regretting being
on the other side when it shuts. But of course she is wholly
subject to our purposes or whims in the matter of the opening
and closing of the doors to the house; I now make a point of
opening doors more frequently, so she need not feel each occasion is so rare or important an opportunity.

I Theresa note further that in encounters with humans, animals rarely have real choices. When an animal indicates her
choice not to interact, her behavior is interpreted as hostile or
as a challenge to conquer. If a human fails to properly interpret
the animal's message and gets hurt, it is the animal who is
punished or even killed. We do not perceive it as an intrusion
for a human to invade an animal's personal space: as women
for men, other animals are always expected to be accessible to
humans. Nor do we often think of the burden our very attention
can be; one is reminded of the justified outrage of women of
color who are forever being asked to represent their group of
origin to "well-meaning" audiences desirous of acquiring en-
lightened attitudes.

The shift—to the extent it has occurred—from hunting animals with guns to hunting them with cameras is not totally
benign. *Hunting* continues, with the same arrogance and domination, as one would expect, given the institutions—oil companies and other corporations notorious for valuing money profits
above the earth and life—that have made nature documentaries the staple of public television viewing. They have made
nature documentaries a rigid and inflexible genre, enforcing the
view that wild species are beings apart, properly confined to
remote (and small) areas of the globe.

Since a predator capturing and feasting on prey seems to be mandatory in every documentary, staged killings are commonplace. Consider the likelihood of a cameraperson happening upon a brilliantly clear, perfectly angled shot of a lion downing a gazelle. As Pat Derby has pointed out, animals cannot act, they do not conjure up emotions on cue. If animals look frightened, it's because they are frightened. A television documentary shown several years ago positively gloried in the ingenious intrusiveness of its methods, proudly detailing the devastation of placing cameras inside nests and dens of animals. No mention of any tidying up or attempts at restoration afterward! Nor any inquiry into the subsequent fate of the particular animals involved.

A recent report in *Sanctuary*, the PAWS newsletter (March 1989), discusses a National Geographic Special (underwritten by Chevron Oil Company) that extols cruel and painful training practices for elephants as the only means of keeping or preserving either the species or individual elephants; despite requests by PAWS, PETA, Cleveland Amory, and others experienced with elephants, the Society refused to consider the inclusion of any alternate practices, or even to admit that any other philosophy of elephant interaction could exist.

Contributing to the widespread U.S. notion of wildlife living apart and elsewhere may be our definition of wildlife as inseparable from the exoticism of tropical regions. Lions and tigers. The great apes. Large, bright-colored birds. Those who live closer to home—coyotes, wolves, mountain lions, eagles—seem not to share the status of lions and tigers though they suffer equal depredation. Often legally categorized as vermin, these and other native species are hunted down by U.S. ranchers with a ferocity scarcely matched by either African farmers or poachers. From the midst of her generally single-minded concern with gorillas, Dian Fossey noted that while only some two hundred and forty mountain gorillas survived, the U.S. population of grizzly bears (excluding Alaska) had dropped to one hundred and eighty-seven. (Some eighteen thousand brown bears, close kin to grizzlies, still live in Europe, primarily in the Balkan region, in close proximity to human settlements and apparently quite peaceably, according to Paul Shepard and Barry Saunders in *The Sacred Paw*.)

The designation *virgin*, applied to wilderness, strikes us as conceptually as arrogant as when applied to women—a definition that rests solely on whether one is used or not by men. It is an illusion to think we live outside nature or that nature is anywhere free of us or able to offer us refuge from ourselves. No ecosystem on earth remains untouched by human activities; nor are we, even in the most dense urban setting, ever outside nature—as evidenced by cockroaches, rats, weeds breaking through asphalt . . . and ourselves. When (white male) explorers talk of being the first to set foot, they are generally referring to places other people and numerous other animals already call home.

The distinction between wilderness and civilization seems particularly meaningless for women, since forests and mountains in fact offer us no greater dangers than those posed by men in cities. In *Women and Wilderness*, Anne La Bastille quotes Maggie Nichols (author of *Wild, Wild Women*):

> the city and the outdoors are similar in many ways. Neither is without its dangers. You have to keep your wits about you all the time—the signs are always there, and you must learn to read them at a glance. In the wilderness, you watch for signals like wildlife and weather; here, for people signs. After all, it is a people place. Both cities and wilderness places demand respect.

She describes bagladies' subculture in cities as comparable to the lives of trappers and hermits in the woods.

There can be neither interaction nor observation without effect; the irresponsible and dangerous myth of "scientific objectivity" is now generally seen as such by scientists, though popular notions lag behind. Effects of human actions need not, however, be harmful. In an essay included in Les Kaufman and Kenneth Mallory's *The Last Extinction*, David Ehrenfeld describes desert habitats in the southwestern United States enriched for birds by small water sources developed by humans for their own use. As Hope Sawyer Buyukmihci documents (in *With a Fly's Eye*), the presence of responsible humans may be the surest protection of wild beings, more effective than our present practice of shading off the intensity of human development through agriculture, which can be more injurious to wildlife than many seemingly more intensely urban activities. The secretive, shy (and endangered) Least Terns nest between the runways of the San Diego Airport. In a poem in the anthology *The Dolphin's Arc*, Anne Mock-Bunting describes humans overseeing egg caches of endangered turtles and guarding hatchlings from human poachers and beach traffic as well as from natural hazards and predators they are no longer sufficiently numerous to support.

Many of our contributors note instances of different animal species living together or meeting harmoniously, with curiosity but not aggression. Perhaps women notice this more than men would; perhaps observers less well trained or less thoroughly assimilated to narrow, scientific ways of thinking notice behaviors outside of the established economic categories for animals of feeding, reproduction, and territorializing, and record observations with more tolerance for a lack of immediate explanation or motivation. Both domestic and wild animals may spend quite a lot of time just hanging out, or checking out their surroundings without any particular aim closely in view; when business they deem important is involved, they may be no more reasoning or restrained than humans in a similar situation.

I Theresa live with a dog, LRB, who always has immediate and intense reactions to people upon first meeting them. She will sometimes growl and other times act quite friendly. After long observation, I have found a pattern in her seemingly unpredictable behavior: she is friendly with people who acknowledge her, who talk to her, rather than to me about her. One could argue, I suppose, that people who don't respond to her directly do so out of fear or dislike for dogs and that LRB is sensing their reactions. It's possible. But what I see is a dog who when treated as an object responds with hostility and when treated as a being responds in kind.

Donna Haraway, who has written in perceptive detail of the colonizing aspect of European and U.S. studies of African animals, believes,

> we are inserted in the web of human social relations even
> when we are alone with animals, even when we are infants
> without speech, even when people never join us in person

in our relationship with animals with whom we bond. I don't agree that there is a pre-social (human social relations) way to relate to animals, domesticated or not. That belief is precisely the one that guides Western people to look for relations with animals outside history. The terms of access to and meaning of the animals are mediated by histories of which we are often unaware. Simultaneously, I think we have deep social relations with animals, a perspective often denied in our culture's frameworks ... (Letter, June 15, 1988).

Pat Derby believes that language interferes with our ability to communicate with other animals, that only through language do we learn we can feel one thing and say its opposite. Nonhuman animals (except perhaps those who are trained to act as humans expect them to act) do not lie. Animals are direct and honest about their wants and needs, likes and dislikes. Communication is transmitted through the whole body. They listen with their eyes and noses and skin and hearts, as well as their ears. To communicate with them requires silence, feeling, moving in tune with them—not imposing on them. Through my work with the animals at the PAWS shelter, I Theresa am learning to speak with my hands and eyes and scent and posture, as well as my voice, and to listen, as they do, with my whole body.

II

Much of the work of this anthology has been, simply, fun: encounters and challenges of the most rewarding sorts. But we have never been free of a nagging sense that the very exceptionalness of our contributors distorts the reality for the overwhelming majority of animals whose lives touch humans—lives, which are, again quite simply, too terrible to bear hearing of. Jean Bilyeu, the domestic animal rescue worker Stephanie interviewed in *With a Fly's Eye*, said:

People say, oh don't tell me about it, I don't want to hear, it makes me sick. That's what's the matter with people. They won't listen. Until they do listen and do get sick nobody's going to do anything. People say, oh I don't want to read it. God damn you, read it! There's too many people ducking the issue in this county. Just yesterday I told Kathleen two instances, of the dog that was hung in the tree and hung there until it choked to death. And the kittens that the man held with their mouths pried open while the kids poured the liquid tar down to see how much they could get in them before they died. And she said, oh that makes me sick. You're goddamn right it makes you sick. So do something about it!

Patricia Curtis, who has spent years developing methods to effectively inform the public about the exploitation of other species, has adopted a different strategy:

If I revealed in my books and articles the immensity of animal suffering, the widespread atrocities committed against them, I'd lose my reader. Because many of my books are written for youngsters, they have to be acceptable to school librarians and teachers, or the kids will never get to read them. Therefore I tone down the facts a bit. While everything I write about is true, I may go easy on the details. It's better to get the news out, to a wide audience, even if I have to break it somewhat gently. (Letter, August 22, 1988)

Coral Lansbury warns in *The Old Brown Dog: Women, Workers, and Vivisection in Edwardian England* of fiction being a double-edged weapon for proponents of social reform: warning of horror and frightening off but also indulging and dissipating emotions. Comedy in particular tends to serve to habituate us to the horrible, to make it more palatable or at least more everyday. Though we had originally hoped to include humorous and comic pieces, we found that, like genre pieces, they generally work more to reinforce than to undercut exploitive stereotypes—indeed, humor often relies precisely on those stereotypes.

Several contributors to the anthology describe encounters with abused draft animals in less technologically developed countries as turning points in the development of their consciousness about animals. (How Art and Life reflect each other: women today reliving this experience that for over a century has been a staple of accounts of white women going out to the colonies, with continuing interplay of the oppression of women, nonwhite persons and nonhuman animals.) We in the United States can hardly pride ourselves on the absence of starving and tortured bullocks and donkeys in our streets; like so much of the understructure of our society, animal abuse is kept out of sight.

It is clear that U.S. society exists on a substratum of animal cruelty—not only the use but the abuse of animals is built into our cultural self-definition, as Carol Adams has explored in several articles (in *With a Fly's Eye* and this volume) and in her book *The Sexual Politics of Meat*. The Western desire to control natural resources and beings—trees, water, animals, women, children, artists, human labor in general—seems always to go beyond economic use (cruel, exploitive, and short-sighted as that often is) to exerting power and domination for their own sake, in ritual displays of destruction.

U.S. agriculture has escalated terror at a pace with our military development. Milk cows no longer graze green fields, but live out their lives as components of industrial machinery. The plight of veal calves has gained some attention (calves being cute); pigs are kept similarly in spaces too small for normal movement, their ears and tails cut off lest they pull them off for lack of anything else to do, risking infection and concomitant expense and inefficiency. Farrowing pens are built over grates through which the piglets fall for convenient removal. The mother cannot be trusted with them—where would she have learned how to mother? How can she be other than crazed and murderous? Laying hens and fryers are packed (in life as in death) several to a small cage, beaks, combs, talons, and other economically nonessential portions of their anatomy removed lest they also injure themselves or each other in a desperate and futile display of self-assertion. Other animals are kept for continuing consumption: ducks plucked thrice during life for down garments; civet cats kept for the produce of their anal glands, used as a fixative in perfumes. Sheep, once kept for the continuing production of wool are now raised primarily for meat; with the lowered demand for wool, sufficient can be had from carcasses.

The women who left the cities in the 1960s for rural farms and communes have now had a good many years of facing, if not coming to terms with, the immediacies of animal (and plant) life (and death) that others of us need consider only when we wish to. A few years ago Sherry Thomas wrote:

> I garden with as much attention as I raise animals. I have seen a columbine I admired and talked to shoot out four more blooms in less than twelve hours, where there had been no buds at all. I have seen a cabbage I was particularly fond of grow twice as big as any other in the row. My experience of plants is that they are as "alive" and sensitive as many animals. I can honestly say that it is sometimes harder for me to pull up a cabbage or cut the heart out of a broccoli plant that I have tended, nourished, and loved, than it is to kill a young rooster that I have no particular relationship to. All eating involved me to some degree or another with killing. ("I Eat Meat," *Country Women,* no. 20)

Jennifer Thiermann writes more recently:

> There are stages that new people in the country seem to go through: the thrill and freedom to have animals, coming face-to-face with the responsibilities and contradictions, and the compromised resolutions (satisfactory and unsatisfactory to my way of thinking). . . . Most women have moved away from animal caretaking and have either moved back to complicated lives in the city or have had to take full-time work in rural towns, therefore having less time for animals and gardening on their homesteads. Our ranch is a wildlife refuge. The other day I was eating lunch, gazing out my window and watching buck deer and a group of ten feral pigs way out in an open meadow. I thought, everyone tells me we should try to get rid of the pigs, but really how many places can they live so exposed and also wild and unafraid. Even if they are not indigenous, it felt right. (Letter, November 5, 1989)

Having now given birth to a child of her own, Jennifer Thiermann feels a newly disturbing sympathy for the dairy goats she once kept, as she remembers taking from them the kids bred solely for the mother's resulting production of milk: "We probably had 175 goats go through our place and I feel we found good homes for only a half a dozen or so."

I Stephanie am not myself—yet—a vegetarian, but the last chicken carcass I bought in a supermarket looked so scrawny and sickly, I had to think the bird had lived in misery, and I have yet to buy another, though I have eaten chickens others put before me. I keep the remains of a steer in the freezer, an animal I first met when he was a few weeks old and watched grow. I do not delude myself that he died willingly or consented to feed me, but the meat is healthy looking, tender and tasty, and I cannot find it in myself to despise the eating of it.

I am bothered by the fact that I do not, and do not wish to, kill to obtain the meat I eat: there is a contradiction I have yet to deal with. Recently I visited the sheep my sister is raising for my eating and her own. Three plump black-faced ewes with lambs huddled in a sunny field, staring back at us, and I thought: they know *something*. They are frightened of us even when we stand here on the other side of the fence, silent and unmoving, only looking at them. Or anyway the knowledge that I would eat them was in the air between them and me, and occluded any other relation that might have been.

I Theresa am choosing for ethical reasons not to eat meat. Unlike friends who have been vegetarians most if not all their lives, I was raised on meat and potatoes. I don't like to eat most vegetables. So I call myself a non-meat-eater rather than a vegetarian and I approach my diet like an addict in recovery—one meal at a time. Keeping living animals in mind helps: I don't allow myself to hide behind euphemisms like "beef" for cow or "pork" for pig. And I appeal to my compassion, rather than placing authoritarian judgement on myself.

I have thought at length about what it is that is wrong about eating flesh and have come to believe there is no inherent wrong in it. What is wrong is subjugating another for the sake of my taste buds, killing someone for something I don't even *need*. If a being dies in his or her own time, I see nothing ethically wrong in consuming the flesh. Or if I were a predator whose survival depended on killing other animals, as many of our ancestors were, facing an equal chance of being hunter or hunted, I would be acting within nature's balance and too could be meat. But neither is what happens in the case of most modern humans eating meat. We are not scavengers or hunters who need to kill; we are predators who have predetermined a "hunt" the other animals have no hope of escaping.

Nor do alternatives to animal sources for food, clothing, and other items come to us without a price in animal suffering. Most synthetic materials are obtained only at considerable cost to the environment, by industries abusive also of human labor. Besides preempting territory where animals previously lived, present-day U.S. monoculture plant raising involves the poisoning with agricultural chemicals of water and what forage remains for wild animals, birds, and insects. Sue Hubbell writes in *A Book of Bees* that one of the greatest risks bees face today is from carrying insecticides home and poisoning their hives. The bluebirds Hope Sawyer Buyukmihci writes of (in *With a Fly's Eye*) are but one of many North American birds that are virtually extinct because of our plant-farming practices; in another generation's time, birds may be a rarity in both the countryside and the cities of the United States.

U.S. flood control and irrigation water projects, particularly in the west and southeast, have altered and destroyed natural habitats and landscapes on a scale that dwarfs the effects of any human war to date. The remaining species of migratory birds in the Western hemisphere continue to be decimated, depending as they do on rapidly shrinking wildlands and marshes while crossing the United States. Many anadromous fish species are already extinct from pollution and poison or impassable dams in the rivers and streams where they spawn. We feel the threat to the salmon fishery of the 1989 Alaska oil spill in part because the once equally rich Atlantic and lower Pacific coast fisheries are so diminished. Susan Maurer, interviewed by Beth Bosk in this volume, notes that on her small stream in northern California, fifty years ago the fall run of Chinook salmon was fifty thousand fish; now they are lucky to get four thousand, and the once equally numerous winter- and spring-running species are extinct. Restaurant menus in the Great Lakes area warn customers it may be hazardous to their health to eat lake fish more than once a week.

Our (generally oversized) houses and workplaces are built from lumber from Western Douglas fir and redwood forests and Southern pine forests, all routinely sprayed with Agent Orange and other defoliants to kill off broadleaf "weed" trees, with expectable results in killing, maiming, and causing birth defects or miscarriage in animals, including humans. Twenty-five years after the publication of Rachel Carson's *Silent Spring*, what was so hotly denied at the time by the poisoners and spoilers is now accepted by industry and public alike as common knowledge—and continues with an ever-escalating assault on the earth and living things.

I Stephanie have been inventorying our kitchen and bathroom shelves: Ivory, Draino, Windex, Spic & Span, Tide, Clorox, Woolite, Easy Off oven cleaner, Pledge furniture polish, Jergens soap and hand lotion, Crest toothpaste, Dry Idea antiperspirant, and Coppertone suntan lotion (it being January, I found that at the back of the shelf). I daresay most of our homes would turn up much the same: household products and cosmetics—and pet products—that are, right now, being tested on living animals.

Lethal dose tests for oral toxicity determine the lethal dose that will kill a given percent of the animals in a test group. Up to two hundred animals may be used in a single test, with the test compound—liquid bleach, for example—force-fed by mouth, through tubes inserted in the animals' throats, by injection, or by forced inhalation. The animals may be dosed daily for months while suffering convulsions, vomiting, diarrhea, paralysis, and bleeding from the eyes, nose, and mouth.

Rabbits are used in the Draize test for eye irritancy because their eyes, unlike ours, do not produce tears that would wash away the test substance. The rabbits are confined in cages that leave only their heads free, and the experimenters drop liquid substances inside the lower eyelid, and then observe the severity of irritation and infection or blindness.

Despite the fact that there is no government requirement for animal testing of cosmetics or household products, and that numerous methods of testing exist that are both less cruel and more reliable (such as computer simulation, cell-culture methods) and that, simplest of all, warning labels could be included on products containing unexpectedly harsh or toxic chemicals, most large U.S. manufacturers routinely retest their existing products on animals as well as all new ones.

Can there be any argument that a new laundry soap or eye shadow justifies even inconvenience to animals let alone torture or death? With consumer demand, "cruelty-free" alternatives are becoming available, though of products commonly offered in most supermarkets, Murphy oil soaps and Bon Ami cleansers are some of the very few that are not, or at least not any longer, tested on animals. More can be purchased by mail order or in natural foods stores and community co-ops. Beauty Without Cruelty has been making cruelty-free cosmetics for many years. Avon and Revlon recently announced that they would cease testing on animals. *Shopping for a Better World*, published by the Council for Economic Priorities, lists hundreds of brand-name products and indicates whether they are tested on animals, as well as the manufacturer's record on such issues as women's rights, the environment, and investment in South Africa.

We make an ethical choice each time we reach for the cleanser on the shelf or walk into a store. We have choices denied laboratory rabbits, mice, and monkeys, and, attending or not, *we do choose*. The quest for politically correct consumption—perhaps a peculiarly U.S. notion to begin with—is obviously illusory: *all* consumption is paid for partly by others, partly with their lives. Like other animals, we humans take what we need to—but how much more? Ingrid Newkirk suggests we ask ourselves as we reach out our hands: Do I need this? Do I really need this? (A lesson put to us again and again by our work on this anthology is that there is no end to what one must question . . . and question.)

As no woman is free while male domination and the threat of assault hangs over any one of us, can any animal be truly secure while he or she is still designated legal property, subject to owners' use and abuse at whim? We are ourselves animals, of course, as nineteenth-century women understood very well when they protested the vivisection of honhuman animals as barely distinct from vivisection of women. John Vyvyan vividly documents in his biographies of Frances Power Cobbe and Anna Kingsford, *In Pity and in Anger*, that as soon as scientists (as it in fact happened, men) started vivisecting animals in the mid-nineteenth century, activists (in fact, women) organized the protests that continue today with organizations like PETA.

The numbers, condition, and fate of the many millions of animals used in medical and other research are secrets kept as securely as those of the offense industry. In many communities pound seizure campaigns have ended the use of stray pets for experimentation, perhaps diluting public interest in the welfare of others less cute, less easily identified with, such as purpose-bred animals like "mini-pigs," already a substantial industry in the United States, as Carol Adams reports (in *With a Fly's Eye*)— creatures brought into existence for the sole purpose of being tormented.

PETA has succeeded in getting the federal government to shut down laboratories at some of the most prestigious universities in the United States for practices that fail to meet even the minimal standards set by law. The vast institutional powers of government, medicine, and the universities have made it clear that they mean to make no changes in their practices and are gearing up to put an end to animal rights groups and advocates by both legal and illegal means.

What does all this add up to? Remembering the gendered organization and eventual dissipation of the community and cohesiveness of the antiwar movement of the 1960s, we feel wary of those who say this or that single issue is paramount and all else must be sacrificed to it. We wonder at environmentalists who establish hierarchies of concern and think an interest in individual animals frivolous sentimentalism; at vegans we have met who treat animals like objects, just not objects they eat. We question the careful, narrowly reasoned rights-based arguments of the (mostly human male) animal rights theorists, enrolling other species one by one as honorary men—a tactic which never accomplished much for women. Much of the "rights" argument persists in linearity and compartmentalization, once again making use of the masculinist mind/body split, separating thought and action from feeling, and valuing the mind over emotions.

For what has ever motivated human action but sentiment? Hope Sawyer Buyukmihci notes (in *With a Fly's Eye*) that a deep love of birds almost always starts with an encounter early in life with one special bird. As Carol McMillan formulates one of the core insights of feminism (in *Women, Reason and Nature*), "To contrast thought and emotion by assuming that the latter is devoid of all cognition is to miss one of its crucial features." It seems to us to be precisely our emotions and sentiments that need cultivation. Marti Kheel gives a practical example:

> If we *think*, for example, that there is nothing morally wrong with eating meat, we ought, perhaps, to visit a factory farm or slaughterhouse to see if we still *feel* the same way. If we, ourselves, do not want to witness, let alone participate in, the slaughter of the animals we eat, we ought, perhaps, to question the morality of indirectly paying someone else to do this on our behalf. When we are physically removed from the direct impact of our moral decisions—i.e., when we cannot see, smell, or hear their results—we deprive ourselves of important sensory stimuli which may be important in guiding us in our ethical choices. ("The Liberation of Nature: A Circular Affair")

In "The Universe Responds," Alice Walker describes her discovery of that responsiveness in the way wildflowers and animals increased around her home after she began to pay attention to them. What you ask, she believes, the Universe will give, and she cites the military-industrial complex as having shown more faith in this regard than "those of us who do not believe in war and who want peace": "They have asked the Earth for all its deadlier substances, [and] the Universe, ever responsive, the Earth, ever giving, has opened itself fully to their desires."

Lewis Thomas observes, in *The Lives of a Cell*, that we are not really individuals even in our own bodies, but colonies and communities of mitochondria and other independent organisms. He finds a tendency in living things to join up, establish linkages, live inside each other, to combine and recombine.

Sally Carrighar (in *With a Fly's Eye*) found ethical guidance in her similar observations:

The responsible care of young, the fidelity of mates if that is the species custom, the respect for others' property, the fairness in taking turns, the rituals that prevent conflicts from being fatal, the lack of malice, the tolerance, the mild-ness of tempers: these are some of the principles of the wilderness code that have insured survival. . . . Once the code was ours. Once we were a species that survived in a wild community, among our animal neighbors. . . . If we are going to try to find our way back to nature's principles, it would seem helpful to rediscover how the animals live. The commandments recognized in the wilderness could be our lifeline to mental and emotional health. . . . But we are apparently bent on destroying the wilderness, which could be the most tragic development in the history of the human race. For if the wilderness is reduced much further, we shall have no clues to nature's moral sanity.

Our work on this anthology has made it indisputably clear to us that animals, for the same reasons and in the same manner as humans, exist each for themselves; that each life in being is "made for" nothing more than to be. Jane Meyerding develops this notion in her review of *With a Fly's Eye* (*Lesbian Contradiction*, Fall 1989):

To be tolerant is to hold oneself apart from the tolerated person(s) or behavior(s). (Or animals.) It's a psychological trick, a sort of mental barrier we erect between ourselves and the "other" in order to restrain our tendency to attack or flee from whatever is different from ourselves. Even the condescending tolerance that labels a person "exotic" be-cause of her culture, or "strong" because of her oppression, or "brave" because she uses a wheelchair is a kind of attack. It's an attempt to avoid the kind of understanding sought by many of the women whose stories are in this anthology, the kind of respectful understanding that can be achieved only if we "sit and be quiet and shut up and stop thinking about what you want them to do" or to be. It takes a hell of a lot of time, a hell of a lot of your life, to even aim for that kind of understanding. And of course, you do risk being changed by the results.

We, Stephanie and Theresa, see that we have been changed in our thoughts, sentiments, and behavior. The different strands of our lives run on, but in each, earth, air, plants, animals grow larger, more vivid, more immediately present. Many confusions and false arguments fall away of themselves as our understanding quickens, and decisions become clearer and easier to make.

I Stephanie still get up in the morning, dress, eat, walk about and write. But I have changed in the clothes I wear and the food I eat and how I eat it, in the paper I write on, the words I write, who I write about and whom I write for. I am more aware of my own life as animal existence; more determined to live my life as an unfragmented whole, and I have learned new ideas of how, in practice, to go about that.

I Theresa have found that animal liberation consciousness, like feminism, resists narrow categorizing as political activity; it is a way of seeing and being in the world. I carry it wherever I go. I've incorporated analysis of the treatment of animals into all the Women's Studies classes I teach, and it fits. We've developed an animal liberation section at the feminist bookstore I own. Likewise I talk feminism to my animal activist friends. As so many pieces in this anthology illustrate—it's all connected. Over the last few months, I've rescued ten ducklings, an opossum, several kittens, a few dogs, and some humans—that work was as important as writing to the president of the United States about the plight of the Silver Springs monkeys, as donating money to save African elephants, as protesting the wearing of furs by those who did not themselves grow them, as compiling these volumes. To merely rescue individual animals without fighting the conditions that put them at risk is like counseling rape victims without teaching them self-defense. But as anyone who ever worked in the anti-rape movement knows, one cannot ignore the needs of individual survivors. It's not a matter of choice; it's a matter of simultaneous attention to ends and means. And when I come home from demonstrating or teaching or selling books, I sit quietly with my animal friends and listen to them—that is part of my political work as well, to pay close attention to what they say.

Each of the writings in this anthology expresses years of a woman's work, thought, and experience with animals. Together, we believe, these poems and stories, articles and interviews add up to a guide for living in the animal world—which is the only world we have. They exemplify and show the results of an ethic of attentiveness, respect, and responsibility—with due skepticism toward our own perception and interpretation. It is a stance that Marilyn Frye articulates in *The Politics of Reality*, as "the loving eye":

The loving eye does not make the object of perception into something edible, does not try to assimilate it, does not reduce it to the size of the seer's desire, fear and imagination, and hence does not have to simplify. It knows the complexity of the other as something which will forever present new things to be known. The science of the loving eye would favor The Complexity Theory of Truth and presuppose The Endless Interestingness of the Universe.

The loving eye seems generous to its object, though it means neither to give nor to take, for not-being-invaded, not-being-coerced, not-being-annexed must be felt in a world such as ours as a great gift.

This work of ours is done . . . on paper. In our selves and lives it has surely only begun, to continue, not always easily or comfortably, toward ends and in ways we as yet may only glimpse. We wish our readers no less as we—and you—turn this last page and continue on in our separate but never again wholly disconnected lives.

Further Reading

Note: This is by no means a complete bibliography of our subject, which would itself fill volumes, but a listing of the writings we found most helpful, or that illustrate or further the work of the contributors to this anthology.

Adams, Carol J. *The Sexual Politics of Meat: A Feminist-Vegetarian Critical Theory.* New York: Continuum, 1990.

Adamson, Joy. *Born Free, A Lioness of Two Worlds.* Reissue of 1960 edition. New York: Random House, 1987.

Allen, Mary. *Animals in American Literature.* Champaign: University of Illinois Press, 1983. (Chapters on animals in U.S. fiction generally and in the poetry of Emily Dickinson and Marianne Moore.)

Anzaldúa, Gloria. *Borderlands/La Frontera: The New Mestiza.* San Francisco: Spinsters/Aunt Lute Book Company, 1987. (Investigates borders between cultures and between species.)

Birke, Lynda. *Women, Feminism and Biology: The Feminist Challenge.* New York: Methuen, 1986.

Boone, J. Allen. *Kinship with All Life.* New York: Harper and Row, 1954. (A manual on communicating with beings from dogs to flies.)
——. *The Language of Silence.* New York: Harper and Row, 1970.

Boulet, Susan Seddon. *Shaman: The Paintings of Susan Seddon Boulet.* San Francisco: Pomegranate, 1989.

Bradley, Marion Zimmer. *Hawkmistress.* New York: DAW Books, 1982. (Novel.)

Brewer, Stella. *The Chimps of Mount Asserik.* New York: Knopf, 1978. (Life in an African forest reintroducing chimpanzees to the wild.)

Butler, Octavia. *Survivor.* Garden City, NY: Doubleday, 1978. (Novel.)

Buyukmihci, Hope Sawyer. *Hour of the Beaver.* Chicago: Rand McNally, 1971.
——. *Unexpected Treasure.* New York: M. Evans and Co., 1968.

Caldecott, Leonie, and Stephanie Leland, eds. *Reclaim the Earth: Women Speak Out for Life on Earth.* London: The Women's Press, 1983.

Cameron, Anne. *Daughters of Copper Woman.* Vancouver, B.C.: Press Gang, 1981.

Cantor, Aviva. "The Club, the Yoke, and the Leash: What We Can Learn from the Way a Culture Treats Animals." *Ms.*, August, 1983.

Carrighar, Sally. *Home to the Wilderness: A Personal Journey.* Boston: Houghton Mifflin, 1973. (Autobiography.)
—— *One Day at Teton Marsh.* Reprint of 1947 edition. Lincoln: University of Nebraska Press, 1979.

——. *One Day on Beetle Rock.* Reprint of 1944 edition. Lincoln: University of Nebraska Press, 1978.
——. *The Twilight Seas: A Blue Whale's Journey.* New York: Weybright and Talley, 1975.
——. *Wild Heritage.* Boston: Houghton Mifflin, 1965.

Carson, Rachel. *The Edge of the Sea.* Boston: Houghton Mifflin, 1955.
——. *The Sea Around Us.* Revision of 1951 edition. New York: Oxford University Press, 1961.
——. *Silent Spring.* Boston: Houghton Mifflin, 1962.
——. *Under the Sea Wind.* New York: Oxford University Press, 1941.

Clark, Eugenie. *Lady with a Spear.* New York: Harper, 1951.

Cohen, Barbara, and Louise Taylor, eds. *Dogs and Their Women.* Boston: Little Brown, 1989. (Photos and brief descriptions of relationships.)

Coleman, Sydney H. *Humane Society Leaders in America.* New York: Humane Association, 1924. (History of women activists and organizers.)

Collard, Andre, and Joyce Contrucci. *The Rape of the Wild.* Bloomington: Indiana University Press, 1989.

Corbo, Margarete Sigl, and Diane Marie Barras. *Arnie and a House Full of Company.* New York: Ballantine, 1989.
——. *Arnie, the Darling Starling.* New York: Ballantine, 1985.

Cornwell-Robinson, Margery, ed. *The Grey Geese: Modern Writings in Honor of Animals.* New York: The Joyce Mertz-Gilmore Foundation, 1985. (Available from the editor, 86 St. James Place, Brooklyn, NY, 11238.)

Corrigan, Theresa, and Stephanie T. Hoppe, eds. *And a Deer's Ear, Eagle's Song, and Bear's Grace: Relationships Between Animals and Women.* San Francisco and Pittsburgh: Cleis Press, 1990.
——. *With a Fly's Eye, Whale's Wit, and Woman's Heart: Relationships Between Animals and Women.* San Francisco and Pittsburgh: Cleis Press, 1989.

Crisler, Lois. *Arctic Wild.* New York: Harper, 1958.

Crounse, Elizabeth. *There Will Be No Ark (An Environmental Distress Call).* New York: Elizabeth Crounse Fine Arts, 1986. (Artist's book with hand-colored plates; signed, numbered copies available from the publisher, 54 Duke Ellington Blvd. #3A, New York, NY 10025.)

Curtis, Patricia. *Animal Doctors.* New York: Delacorte, 1977.
——. *Animal Partners: Training Animals To Help People.* New York: Lodestar Books, 1982
——. *Animal Rights.* New York: Four Winds/MacMillan, 1980.
——. *The Animal Shelter.* New York: Lodestar Books, 1984.
——. *Dogs on the Case: Search Dogs Who Help Save Lives and Enforce the Law.* New York: Lodestar Books, 1989.
——. *The Indoor Cat.* New York: Perigree, 1981.
——. *The Urban Dog.* New York: Bantam, 1986.

Dawkins, Marian Stamp. *Animal Suffering: The Science of Animal Welfare*. London: Chapman and Hall, 1980. (An investigation of the needs and preferences of battery chickens and other factory-farmed animals.)

Derby, Pat (with Peter S. Beagle). *The Lady and her Tiger.* Reprint of 1976 Ballantine edition $8.00 ppd. from Lioness Books, 2224 J Street, Sacramento, CA 95816.

Ehrlich, Paul and Anne. *Extinction.* New York: Random House, 1981.

Elia, Irene. *The Female Animal.* New York: Henry Holt, 1988.

Elston, Mary Ann, "Women and Anti-Vivisection in Victorian England," *Vivisection in Historical Perspective*, Nicolas A. Rupke, ed. New York: Methuen, 1987.

Engel, Marian. *Bear.* New York: Atheneum, 1976. (Novel.)

Facklam, Margery. *Wild Animals, Gentle Women.* New York: Harcourt Brace Jovanovich, 1978. (Profiles of eleven women who work with or study wild animals.)

Ferris, Chris. *The Darkness Is Light Enough: The Field Journal of a Night Naturalist.* New York: The Ecco Press, 1988.

Fossey, Dian. *Gorillas in the Mist.* Boston: Houghton Mifflin, 1983.

Gawain, Elizabeth. *The Dolphin's Gift.* Mill Valley, CA: Whatever Publishing, 1981. (On visiting free-living dolphins in Australia.)

Gearhart, Sally Miller. *The Wanderground: Stories of the Hill Women.* Boston: Alyson Publications, 1984.

George, Jean Craighead. *Journey Inward.* New York: Dutton, 1982.

Goodall, Jane. *In the Shadow of Man.* Boston: Houghton Mifflin, 1971.

Grahn, Judy. *Mundane's World.* Freedom, CA: The Crossing Press, 1988. (Novel.)

Grandin, Temple, and Margaret M. Scariano. *Emergence: Labeled Autistic.* Novato, CA: Arena Press, 1986. (The life and recovery of an autistic child who now works as an engineer designing humane livestock and slaughterhouse facilities.)

Griffin, Susan. *Made from This Earth.* New York: Harper and Row, 1982.
———. *Woman and Nature: The Roaring Inside Her.* New York: Harper and Row, 1978.

Haraway, Donna. *Primate Visions: Gender, Race and Nature in the World of Modern Science.* New York: Routledge, 1989.
———. *Simians, Cyborgs, and Women: The Reinvention of Nature.* London: Free Association Books, 1990.

Harrison, Ruth. *Animal Machines.* London: Vincent Stuart, 1964. (The classic study and exposé of factory farming.)

Harrisson, Barbara. *Orang-utan.* New York: Doubleday, 1963. (Reintroducing orangutans to the wild.)

Hearne, Vicki. *Adam's Task: Calling Animals by Name.* New York: Knopf, 1986.

Hickford, Jessie. *Eyes at My Feet.* New York: St. Martin's Press, 1973. (A blind woman's account of life with a seeing-eye dog.)

Hocken, Sheila. *Emma and I.* New York: Dutton, 1977. (A blind woman's account of life with a seeing-eye dog.)

Holland, Barbara. *Secrets of the Cat: Its Lore, Legend, and Lives.* Reprint of *The Name of the Cat.* New York: Ballantine, 1989.

Hoover, Helen. *The Gift of the Deer.* New York: Knopf, 1973. (Life in the Minnesota North Woods.)
———. *The Long-Shadowed Forest.* New York: Crowell, 1963.
———. *A Place in the Woods.* New York: Knopf, 1969.
———. *The Years of the Forest.* New York: Knopf, 1973.

Hoppe, Stephanie T. *The Windrider.* New York: DAW Books, 1985. (Novel.)

Hrdy, Sarah Blaffer. "Empathy, Polyandry, and the Myth of the Coy Female," *Feminist Approaches to Science,* Ruth Bleier, ed. New York: Pergamon, 1986. (A female scientist's inquiry into the evolutionary strategies of the sexes.)

Hubbell, Sue. *A Book of Bees . . . And How To Keep Them.* New York: Ballantine, 1988.
———. *A Country Year: Living the Questions.* New York: Harper and Row, 1987.

Hynes, H. Patricia. *The Recurring Silent Spring.* New York: Pergamon, 1989. (On Rachel Carson and the outcome of her work, by an environmental engineer.)

Johnson, Buffie. *Lady of the Beasts: Ancient Images of the Goddess and Her Sacred Animals.* San Francisco: Harper and Row, 1988. (With extensive illustrations of prehistoric and historic art and artifacts.)

Johnson, Sally Patrick, ed. *Everyman's Ark: A Collection of True First-Person Accounts of Relationships Between Animals and Men.* New York: Harper and Brothers, 1962. (Includes a few women.)

Kheel, Marti. "The Liberation of Nature: A Circular Affair," *Environmental Ethics* 7:2 (Summer 1985). (Feminist analysis of academic environmental ethics.)

Kolodny, Annette. *The Land Before Her: Fantasy and Experience of the American Frontiers, 1630–1860.* Chapel Hill: University of North Carolina Press, 1984. (White women's responses to the American frontier and wilderness.)

Kumin, Maxine. *In Deep: Country Essays.* Boston: Beacon, 1988.

La Tourette, Aileen. *Cry Wolf.* London: Virago Press, 1986. (Novel.)

LaBastille, Anne. *Assignment: Wildlife*. New York: Dutton, 1980.
———. *Beyond Black Bear Lake*. New York: Norton, 1987.
———. *Women and Wilderness*. San Francisco: Sierra Club Books, 1980.
———. *Woodswoman*. New York: Dutton, 1976.

Lansbury, Coral. *The Old Brown Dog: Women, Workers and Vivisection in Edwardian England*. Madison: University of Wisconsin Press, 1985.

Le Guin, Ursula K. *Always Coming Home*. New York: Harper and Row, 1985. (Novel.)
———. *Buffalo Gals and Other Animal Presences*. Santa Barbara, CA: Capra Press, 1987. (Short fiction and poetry.)
———. *Dancing at the Edge of the World*. New York: Grove Press, 1989. (Essays.)

Lessing, Doris. *Particularly Cats*. New York: Simon and Schuster, 1967.

Linden, Eugene. *Silent Partners: The Legacy of the Ape Language Experiments*. New York: Times Books, 1986.

Lynch, Lee. *Sue Slate, Private Eye*. Tallahassee, FL: Naiad, 1989. (Novel.)

Mazza, Cris. *Animal Acts*. New York: Fiction Collective, 1989. (Short fiction.)

McCaffrey, Anne. *Dragonflight*. New York: Ballantine, 1968. (Novel.)

McIntyre, Joan, ed. *Mind in the Waters: A Book to Celebrate the Consciousness of Whales and Dolphins*. San Francisco: Sierra Club Books, 1974. (Poetry, personal experience, natural history.)

McIntyre, Vonda N. *Dreamsnake*. New York: Dell, 1978. (Novel.)
———. *Fireflood and Other Stories*. New York: Pocket Books, 1979.

McMullen, Jeanine. *My Small Country Living*. New York: Warner Books, 1984.

Merchant, Carolyn. *The Death of Nature: Women, Ecology and the Scientific Revolution*. San Francisco: Harper and Row, 1980.

Midgley, Mary. *Animals and Why They Matter*. Athens: University of Georgia Press, 1984. (Excellent summary of Western philosophical traditions as they relate to the causes of and remedies for the abuse of animals, and relationships between the status of animals and women.)
———. *Beast and Man*. Ithaca, NY: Cornell University Press, 1978.

Mooney, Samantha. *Snowflake in My Hand*. New York: Delacorte, 1983. (Work with cats in a large veterinary hospital.)

Moran, Victoria. *Compassion: The Ultimate Ethic*. Wellingtonborough, Northampshire: Thorsons Publishers, 1985.

Moss, Cynthia. *Elephant Memories: Thirteen Years in the Life of an Elephant Family*. New York: Morrow, 1988.

"Nature." *Women of Power* Special Issue, Spring 1988. (Includes bibliography and lists of organizations, cruelty-free products, and manufacturers who test products on animals.)

New Settler Interview. Bioregional newsprint magazine covering northern California. $10.00/twelve issues. P.O. Box 702, Mendocino, CA 95460.

Nice, Margaret Morse. *Research is a Passion with Me.* Toronto: Consolidated Amethyst Communications, 1979. (Autobiography.)
———. *The Watcher at the Nest.* New York: Macmillan, 1939. (First life cycle studies of birds in the U.S.)

Nollman, Jim. *Animal Dreaming: The Art and Science of Interspecies Communication.* New York: Bantam Books, 1987.

Owens, Mark and Delia. *Cry of the Kalahari.* Boston: Houghton Mifflin, 1984. (Wife and husband wildlife observation team.)

Pearson, Jean. *On Speaking Terms with Earth.* Rexville, NY: Great Elm Press, 1988. (Poetry.)

Personal Care with Principle: A Guide to Choosing Cruelty-Free Cosmetics and Products from Major Manufacturers. Available from The National Anti-Vivisection Society, 53 West Jackson Blvd., Suite 1550, Chicago, IL 60604.

Plant, Judith, ed. *Healing the Wounds: The Promise of Ecofeminism.* Santa Cruz, CA: New Society Publishers, 1989.

Rasa, Anne. *Mongoose Watch: A Family Observed.* London: John Murry, 1985. (Details social relations and language of free-living dwarf mongooses and their interactions with other species.)

Richards, Dorothy, with Hope Sawyer Buyukmihci. *Beaversprite: My Years Building an Animal Sanctuary.* Interlaken, NY: Heart of the Lakes Publishing, 1983.

Ritchie, Elisavietta, ed. *The Dolphin's Arc: Poems on Endangered Creatures of the Sea.* College Park, MD: SCOP Publications, 1989.

Rowell, Thelma. *The Social Behavior of Monkeys.* New York: Penguin, 1973. (One of the early woman field observers to make the then revolutionary discovery that female animals exhibit interesting and observable behavior.)

Ryden, Hope. *America's Last Wild Horses.* New York: Dutton, 1970. (Thorough account of history and present plight of wild horses in U.S.)
———. *God's Dog.* New York: Coward, McCann and Geoghegan, 1975. (Excellent study of coyotes.)
———. *Lily Pond.* New York: Morrow, 1989. (Observations of beavers.)
———. *Mustangs: A Return to the Wild.* New York: Viking, 1972. (A book of photographs.)

Salamone, Constantia. "The Prevalence of the Natural Law Within Women: Women and Animal Rights," *Reweaving the Web of Life,* Pam McAllister, ed. Philadelphia: New Society Publishers, 1982.

Sarton, May. *The Fur Person.* New York: Rinehart, 1957.

Schleifer, Harriet. "Images of Death and Life: Food Animal Production and the Vegetarian Option," *In Defense of Animals,* Peter Singer, ed. New York: Harper and Row, 1986.

Sewell, Anna. *Black Beauty.* Originally published in 1877. Chicago: Rand Mc-Nally, 1983. (Best-selling animal rights novel.)

Shaw, Evelyn, and Joan Darling. *Female Strategies.* New York: Touchstone, 1985.

Slonczewski, Joan. *A Door into Ocean.* New York: Avon, 1986. (Novel.)

Small, Meredith F., ed. *Female Primates: Studies by Women Primatologists.* Volume 4, Monographs in Primatology. New York: Alan R. Liss, 1984.

Spiegel, Marjorie. *The Dreaded Comparison: Race and Animal Slavery.* Introduction by Alice Walker. Santa Cruz, CA: New Society Publishers, 1989.

Strom, Deborah, ed. *Birdwatching with American Women: A Selection of Nature Writings.* New York: Norton, 1986. (Excellent anthology of nineteenth- and early-twentieth-century writings by amateur and professional nature observers; also covers the early nature education and conservation movements.)

Strum, Shirley. *Almost Human: A Journey into the World of Baboons.* New York: Random House, 1987.

TallMountain, Mary. *There is No Word for Goodbye.* Marvin, SD: Blue Cloud Abbey Press, 1982; reissue forthcoming Palo Alto, CA: Open Heart Press, 1990. (Poetry.)

Thomas, Elizabeth Marshall. *Reindeer Moon.* Boston: Houghton Mifflin, 1987. (Novel.)

Tyson, Jon-Wynne, compiler. *The Extended Circle: A Commonplace Book of Animal Rights.* New York: Paragon House, 1985.

Vyvyan, John. *In Pity and in Anger.* Reprint of 1969 edition. Marblehead, MA: Micah Publications, 1988. (Biographies of the the nineteenth-century antivivisectionists, Frances Power Cobbe and Anna Kingsford.)
———. *The Dark Face of Science.* London: Michael Joseph, 1969. (History of the antihumane bias of twentieth-century science.)

Webb, Mary. *Gone to Earth.* Reprint of 1917 edition. Wolfeboro, NH: Longwood, 1978. (Novel.)

Whitely, Opal. *The Singing Creek Where the Willows Grow.* Presented by Benjamin Hoff. New York: Warner Books, 1986.

Will, Rosalyn, Alice Tepper Marlin, and Benjamin Corson. *Shopping for a Better World: A Quick and Easy Guide to Socially Responsible Supermarket Shopping.* New York: The Council on Economic Priorities, 1989.

Woolf, Virginia. *Flush.* New York: Harcourt, 1933. (Biography of Elizabeth Barrett Browning's dog Flush.)

Zahava, Irene, ed. *Through Other Eyes: Animal Stories by Women.* Freedom, CA: The Crossing Press, 1988.

zana. *herb womon.* $4.00 ppd. from the author, 12150 w. calle seneca, tucson, az 85743. (Lesbian-feminist poetry and art.)

Contributors' Notes

Janet E. Aalfs lives in the Pioneer Valley of western Massachusetts, where she practices and teaches martial arts. She is a founding member of two lesbian writing groups, and her poetry and prose have been published in women's publications and anthologies. One of her guardian spirits is a seal.

Carol J. Adams is the author of *The Sexual Politics of Meat: A Feminist-Vegetarian Critical Theory* (1990), which won the First Annual Continuum Women's Studies Award.

Dori Appel is a playwright, poet, and fiction writer as well as a clinical psychologist in Ashland, OR. She is co-founder and co-director of "Mixed Company," a theater company dedicated to original works of social and feminist importance, in which she frequently performs. She wrote "A Double Life" for a national horse poetry contest.

Diane de Avalle-Arce is a fugitive from teaching and the East Coast. She has published scholarly work as well as a few prize-winning short stories; her fantasy novel *Calabrinia Falling* will be published by The Crossing Press this year. She presently lives in California, on the edge of the San Rafael Mountains, where she often sneaks away on horseback.

Judith Barrington is the author of *History and Geography* (1989) and *Trying to be an Honest Woman* (1985), both published by The Eighth Mountain Press, and the founder of The Flight of the Mind summer writing workshop for women. She was born and raised in England and now lives in Portland, OR.

Beth Bosk is the editorial voice of *New Settler Interview*, a bioregional newsprint magazine covering the coastal dwellers and hill peoples of northern California in the belief that people have sufficient attention spans.

Frances Burton has spent two decades watching monkeys cavort, gambol, politic, love, and die in Africa, Gibraltar, and most recently, Kowloon, Hong Kong, where she completed a thirty-minute video, "The Monkeys of Kowloon," for a general audience. The mother of twin daughters, she lives in Canada in the country with a diversified assemblage of remarkable barnyard creatures.

Chrystos, a Native American, was born in 1946 and raised in San Francisco; she presently lives on Bainbridge Island, WA. A political activist and speaker as well as an artist and writer, she is self-educated. Her work is directed at better understanding how colonialism, genocide, class, and gender affect the lives of women and Native people.

Jane Curry is the author of *The River's in My Blood: Riverboat Pilots Tell Their Stories*. She has also edited an anthology of Marietta Holley's humor, entitled *Samantha Rastles the Woman Question*, and travels nationally and internationally performing her one-woman show by the same name.

Lorraine Dale works as an actress and singer in repertory theater, with the goal of eventually performing her own original material. She is presently touring with the national company of *Les Misérables*.

Amy Edgington is a disabled Lesbian artist and writer from the South. Her poetry has appeared in *Common Lives/Lesbian Lives*.

Margo Gathright-Dietrich shares a cottage in the woods of Virginia with her husband, two dogs, and a wary orange tabby named Tigger.

Sally Miller Gearhart is a writer, professor, and activist for animal rights, lesbian/gay and women's rights, and in solidarity with Nicaragua Libre. She is the author of *The Wanderground: Stories of the Hill Women* and *A Feminist Tarot* (with Susan Rennie); she has appeared in two films, "The Life and Times of Harvey Milk" and "The Word is Out."

Linda Hogan is a Chickasaw writer with international recognition for her poetry and short fiction. She is the recipient of a National Endowment for the Arts grant and has served on the NEA poetry panel. Her first novel, *Mean Spirit,* will be published this year by Knopf. She has taught writing to students of all ages and is involved in wildlife rehabilitation as a volunteer.

Jeane Jacobs was born in 1947 in Muskogee County, OK, of the Bird Clan, of Choctaw-Cherokee and Irish heritage. "Wings" comes from her own vision quest. She believes that humans and animals make up the pieces of the whole, like grains of sand on the beach. She works as a highway landscape inspector and writes to "stay alive."

Denise Levertov was born in England in 1923 and was educated at home. She studied ballet and, during the Second World War, worked as a nurse. She moved to the United States in 1948, teaching as well as publishing numerous collections of poetry and essays.

Jean Pearson, a poet, editor, translator, and animal rights advocate from Bethlehem, PA, edited the special "Earth" issue of the Walt Whitman Association's *Mickle Street Review* (1985). Her poetry has appeared in periodicals and anthologies and a collection, *On Speaking Terms with Earth* (1988). She has recently compiled an anthology of tales, poetry, and essays on the wolf, her spirit animal.

Marge Piercy has published ten novels, eleven collections of poetry, and a collection of essays as well as edited an anthology of women's poetry, *Early Ripening*. She travels extensively, giving readings and lectures, and otherwise lives with her husband on Cape Cod.

Elisavietta Ritchie's books include *Tightening the Circle Over Eel Country,* winner of the Great Lakes Colleges Association's New Writer's Award for Best First Book of Poetry. She is thrice a PEN Syndicated Fiction winner and editor of *The Dolphin's Arc: Poems on Endangered Creatures of the Sea*. She also translates Russian and French and teaches. She lives in Washington, D.C. and by the Patuxent River.

Alix Kates Shulman has written four novels, two books on Emma Goldman, books for children, and numerous stories and essays. She has been a visiting artist at the American Academy in Rome and received a National Endowment for the Arts Fellowship in fiction.

Susan Stinson lives in a cabin in the woods near Williamsburg, MA, where she is completing a novel entitled *Chalcedony*.

Mary TallMountain, of Koyukon Athabascan Russian Celtic origin, was born in the Alaska Territory in 1918. Her poetry has appeared in numerous anthologies and a collection, *There is No Word for Goodbye.* She has in progress a novel set in Alaska, devoted, like much of her other work, to social insights.

Alison Townsend is a poet and essayist, temporarily displaced from the Pacific Northwest to Madison, WI. Her work has appeared in many small press publications. "Leaving Dorland Mountain" was inspired by her residence as a Fellow at Dorland Mountain Colony.

Pamela Uschuk's poems have appeared in numerous journals and anthologies and won prizes from, among others, the National Poetry Competition sponsored by the Chester H. Jones Foundation. She presently teaches creative writing at Green Haven Maximum Security Prison and serves as Poet in Public Service in New York.

Brenda Weathers lives on an island in Puget Sound and shares her life with two dogs, four cats, and a bunny—all previously homeless. She is the author of several short stories published by local and lesbian/feminist presses and a novel, *The House at Pelham Falls* (1985).

Barbara J. Wood lives in Columbus, OH, with her husband, horse, two cats, and cotherapist, Holly. She completed her Ph.D. with a dissertation on discrimination against women in death and dying and remains involved in feminism as well as animal-assisted therapies, including therapeutic horseback riding.

Organizations and Resources

For organizations in your area contact People for the Ethical Treatment of Animals or United Animal Nations-USA.

People for the Ethical Treatment of Animals
P.O. Box 42516
Washington, DC 20077
(Will send literature about companies that do and do not use animal products or test on animals)

United Animal Nations-USA
P.O. Box 188890
Sacramento, CA 95818
(Their goal is to unite the whole humane movement)

Feminists for Animal Rights
P.O. Box 10017, North Berkeley Sta.
Berkeley, CA 94709

About the Editors

Theresa Corrigan's life has always been a montage of furred, feathered, and finned friends—from earliest memories of a farm near Philadelphia where she lived with her family of three humans, thirty-five cats (all named and known), Smokey Dog, chickens, cows, and countless "saved" rabbits, mice, and birds to her current household of several cats, and dogs, and dozens of fish. Neighbors call her "the weird cat lady on the corner" and vagabond animals know her as a reliable meal ticket.

She teaches Women's Studies at California State University, Sacramento, owns and operates Lioness Books, the local feminist bookstore, and writes. She also volunteers at the PAWS animal shelter and counts among her friends a baboon, a lioness, a baby elephant, and several bears. It was Sweet William, an old black bear, who first encouraged her to work on this anthology.

Stephanie T. Hoppe is a native of the coastal hill country of northern California. A lawyer, she worked for five years in the field of regulating the development of natural resources, in the course of which she came to see the starting point for such work lies in our ideas and expectations of the world, and she turned to writing fiction. Her novel *The Windrider*, sf/fantasy grounded in the myths and landscapes of the North American West, was published in 1985. She is presently completing *If Mirrors Asked Questions*, a collection of linked novellas set in different futures.

To finance the above, she works as a free-lance editor, copyeditor, and proofreader. She also makes wine, raises vegetables, and studies t'ai chi ch'uan, while attempting to reconcile her ambitions to both step lightly on the earth and put her mark upon the world.